A Guide to Leadership and Management in Higher Education

A Guide to Leadership and Management in Higher Education explores an innovative approach to supervision, leadership, and management in the higher education workplace. Drawing from humanism and positive psychology, Fitch and Van Brunt weave together a compelling narrative for managing employees across generational differences. This book shares key leadership lessons to inspire creativity, increase efficiency, and tap into the talents of your diverse, multi-generational staff. Readers will find practical and detailed advice on establishing new relationships, setting expectations, encouraging accountability, addressing conflict, and supervising difficult staff. Focusing on how to build and strengthen connections through genuineness and empathic caring, this book provides important guidance for today's college and university leaders.

Poppy Fitch is the Associate Vice President of Student Affairs at Ashford University, USA.

Brian Van Brunt is a Vice President at the NCHERM Group, USA.

D1598424

A Guide to Leadership and Management in Higher Education

Managing Across the Generations

Poppy Fitch and
Brian Van Brunt

Routledge
Taylor & Francis Group

NEW YORK AND LONDON

First published 2016
by Routledge
711 Third Avenue, New York, NY 10017

and by Routledge
2 Park Square, Milton Park, Abingdon, Oxon, OX14 4RN

Routledge is an imprint of the Taylor & Francis Group, an informa business

© 2016 Taylor & Francis

The right of Poppy Fitch and Brian Van Brunt to be identified as authors of this work has been asserted by them in accordance with sections 77 and 78 of the Copyright, Designs and Patents Act 1988.

Library of Congress Cataloging in Publication Data
Names: Fitch, Poppy, author. | Van Brunt, Brian, author.
Title: A guide to leadership and management in higher education : managing across the generations / Poppy Fitch and Brian Van Brunt.
Description: New York, NY : Routledge, 2016. | Includes bibliographical references and index.
Identifiers: LCCN 2015041567 (print) | LCCN 2016002626 (ebook) |
ISBN 9781138913158 (hardback) | ISBN 9781138913172 (pbk.)
| ISBN 9781315691596 (ebk) | ISBN 9781315691596 (eBook)
Subjects: LCSH: Universities and colleges--Administration. |
Education, Higher--Administration. | Educational leadership.
Classification: LCC LB2341 .F498 2016 (print) | LCC LB2341 (ebook) |
DDC 378.1/01--dc23LC record available at http://lccn.loc.gov/2015041567

ISBN: 978-1-138-91315-8 (hbk)
ISBN: 978-1-138-91317-2 (pbk)
ISBN: 978-1-315-69159-6 (ebk)

Typeset in Sabon and Bell Gothic
by Saxon Graphics Ltd, Derby

Brian's Dedication

To my sexy, brilliant, outspoken wife:
Your support, love, grace and patience lift me to great heights and accomplishments. I couldn't do any of this without you.

Also, thanks for the door.

Poppy's Dedication

To Amiee, Amber, and Sheri:
Thank you for being living, breathing examples of strong women of integrity, for showing me opportunity, and for believing in me when I found it difficult to believe in myself.

To my Millennial and Gen Z young people, Hannah and Kat:
May your paths to discovering your meaning lead you directly to your life's work.

To Mike:
You make everything easier, and I love you for it.

I suppose the most revolutionary act one can engage in is ... to tell the truth.

Howard Zinn, *Marx in Soho: A Play on History*

And now here is my secret, a very simple secret: It is only with the heart that one can see rightly; what is essential is invisible to the eye.

Antoine de Saint-Exupéry, *The Little Prince*

Greatness is a transitory experience. It is never consistent. It depends in part upon the myth-making imagination of humankind. The person who experiences greatness must have a feeling for the myth he is in. He must reflect what is projected upon him. And he must have a strong sense of the sardonic. This is what uncouples him from belief in his own pretensions. The sardonic is all that permits him to move within himself. Without this quality, even occasional greatness will destroy a man.

Frank Herbert, *Dune*

Some people care too much. I think it's called love.

A.A. Milne, *Winnie-the-Pooh*

Contents

Preface

We are sincerely grateful for the opportunity to write *A Guide to Leadership and Management in Higher Education: Managing Across the Generations*, seeing it as an opportunity to share some of the practical and spiritual leadership lessons we have learned in leading our teams, in being led, and learning from our colleagues around the United States. We were inspired to write this book by intersecting motivations. Primarily, we understand the critical difference a changing narrative can make.

With more than three decades of higher education leadership experience between us, we'd heard—and had told—many stories of frustration with our own staff and the staff of colleagues, around workplace preferences, priorities and values. One of the dimensions we noticed coming up again and again was that of generational differences. We have all been guilty of making the mistake of allowing stereotyped ideas about staff (and students!) limit our ability to be effective as leaders, and we invite your self-reflection on this topic.

An additional focus of the book is an assertion that shifting our way of leadership to one that stresses the primacy of the relationship can indeed change the narrative. Here, we introduce the concept of bringing four letter words to work: love, care, and hope. We offer examples of systems where these very concepts contribute to a changing landscape, and challenge the reader to consider their own values as they relate to these particular four letter words, and their application in the workplace.

It is sincerely our hope that this text will be a useful manual for the reader to undertake as they wish—in a single read, or by referencing the chapters as they call to you. The text includes a variety of elements. *Part I: A New Way of Thinking* outlines an argument for a schema shift from a more distant and cognitive leadership and management style, to one that strives to build and strengthen connection through genuineness, congruence and empathic caring. Beyond acknowledging the differing generational idiosyncrasies with tolerance, we invite our readers to consider a strength-based approach that clears the way for leaders to tap into the talents of their diverse, multi-generational staff. *Part II: Putting It Into Practice* provides practical guidance for establishing a new relationship, holding staff accountable and addressing potential conflict from a love-based perspective. Through the use of case studies that bridge the generations, we demonstrate core concepts in addressing conflict, finding common ground, setting expectations and encouraging accountability in order to capitalize on the strengths of your staff.

In *Examples from the Experts* in Chapters 4, 5 and 10, we share our own—and invite other higher education leaders to share their own—narratives of leadership experiences and observations related to the topics introduced in each chapter. It is our belief that stories bring us together. The power of stories and the importance of wisdom-sharing is evidenced in the ripple from one leader to the next. We invite you to find the connections here.

In Chapters 8 and 9—*Addressing Common Staff Problems* and *Avoiding Common Supervisor Mistakes*—you will find and explore case studies that we hope you will use in your own development, and as a starting point to spark critical questions and discussions. The case study approach is used to highlight the commonly encountered staff problems in a manner that allows staff to put themselves into the perspective of the supervisor trying to bring about change. While this style marks a departure from that of the rest of the book, we felt this was a useful way to help our readers wrestle with the practical challenges of putting the concepts outlined in the previous chapters into practice. As with most scenarios, you may find yourself nodding in agreement or even inserting the name of a member of your staff who is reminiscent of a particular case study. Go with it!

A favorite movie of the authors is *City Slickers*, starring Billy Crystal. A recurrent theme in the movie is Curly, the cowboy played by the inimitable Jack Palance, telling Crystal's character Mitch to find that "one thing." The concept of elegance in simplicity as a grounding force for leaders sharing their one guiding principle can be found in science in Occam's Razor, the problem-solving principle with a preference for simplicity. In contemporary music, one might look to Jewel's modest lyric, "What's simple is true."

The *Just One Thing* feature found in every chapter throughout the book was born from this universal principle, and inspired us to ask those in leadership positions across higher education to think about their "one thing" when it came to leadership. It is our hope that there are some useful gems of wisdom in this collection of guiding principles for those in leadership positions across the country. We invite you to reflect, be inspired and perhaps even challenged by what you find in them.

Finally, *Key Take-a-ways* will help to synthesize the concepts explored within each chapter. They are the CliffsNotes of the text (only Xers and older will understand this reference—Millennials will need to Google it). You're welcome.

In a moment of self-awareness, we recognized that our own Gen X biases for respect, diversity, justice, flexibility, informality, and work/life balance will come through in the way we approach this work. In particular, this will be clear in our own *Examples from the Experts*. It is possible that you will find out more about Gen Xers by simply reading a text on Leadership in Higher Education written by two Gen Xers. We invite you to indulge and enjoy this perspective as its own learning experience.

Acknowledgments

We would like to acknowledge with gratitude the contributions made to this work by our colleagues in the profession. Their voices lend to the rich tapestry of this text to ensure readers hear from Mature and Boomer senior leaders, and from Gen X and Millennial next generation-leaders. It is only with their help that we were able to create a work that brings practical application to this text.

With our thanks to our *Example from the Expert* contributors:

Aimee Slade, M.A., Associate Director of Quality Assurance, Office of the Registrar, Ashford University

Aaron W. Hughey, Ed.D., Professor and Program Coordinator, Department of Counseling and Student Affairs, Western Kentucky University

Adrienne C. Brown, Career Center Director, UMOJA Director/Counselor, Los Angeles Harbor College

David J. Denino, Director Emeritus, Counseling Services, Southern Connecticut State University

Laura E. Ulmer, M.Ed., Director of Student Conduct & Academic Integrity, Old Dominion University

Richard Pattenaude, Ph.D., President and CEO, Ashford University

Charlita Shelton, Ph.D., Past President & CEO, University of the Rockies

Peggy S. Scott, Ed.D., LPC-S, Director, Student Rights and Responsibilities Office, Stephen F. Austin State University

Jason Buck, Associate Dean of Students, New England College

Maria Nieto-Senour, Ph.D., President, San Diego Community College District Board of Trustees, Emeritus Professor and Former Program Director, Community Based Block, Department of Counseling and School Psychology, San Diego State University

Eileen Piersa, M.S., M.A., Director of Education Operations and Campus Relations, Institute for Palliative Care, Cal State University, San Marcos

Ron Gaschler, Associate Director, Career Services, University of Arizona

Kyle Robinson, Higher Education Consultant, formerly of the Gallup Organization

Tamara Small, Career Services Manager, Ashford University

Sara Headden, Job Developer/Internship Coordinator, San Diego City College

Genesis Lastrella-Quicho, Career Services Specialist, Ashford University

Steve Salter, M.Ed., Director, Student Access and Wellness, Ashford University

Dr. Amy Murphy, Dean of Students, Texas Tech University

Juan Camarena, Ph.D., Program Director and Lecturer, Community Based Block Co-Director, Center for Community Counseling and Engagement, San Diego State University

Jessica Riley, M.A., Associate Director, Disability Services, University of Denver

With our thanks to our *Just One Thing* contributors:

Josh E. Gunn, Ph.D., Executive Director, Counseling and Psychological Services, Kennesaw State University

Erika Saracino, Clery Compliance Officer, University of California, San Diego

Lisa Medina, M.B.A., CFE, Associate University Registrar & Director of Student Records, Ashford University

Nola Butler-Byrd, Ph.D., LPCC, Associate Professor, Community-Based Block Program Director, Department of Counseling & School Psychology, College of Education, San Diego State University

Greg Elliott, M.A., LPC, Director, Counseling & Career Services, Adams State University

Jacquie Furtado, M.Ed., Associate Vice President, Strategy Management & Engagement, Ashford University

Dr. Mitchell A. Levy, Vice President of Student Affairs & Branch Campus Management, Atlantic Cape Community College

David J. Denino, LPC, NCC, Director Emeritus, Counseling Services, Adjunct Professor, Clinical Mental Health Program, Southern Connecticut State University

Amber Eckert, Vice President, Student Services, Alliant International University

Charles R. Minnick, Ph.D., Vice President/Campus Director, Ashford University
Dr. Chip Reese, Assistant Vice President for Student Affairs & Dean of Students, Columbus State University
Linda Rawles, J.D., C.C.E.P., Rawles Law

We are sincerely grateful,
Poppy and Brian

Linda Rawles, J.D., C.C.E.P.
Rawles Law

My "one thing" is integrity. When I taught ethics for a decade, I would insist that my students identify and define their values, turn those values into principles, and arrange those principles into an ethical framework. It was a bit legalistic, but it worked, teaching them both ethics and critical thinking skills.

It always bothered me when people used "integrity" without defining it, but maybe they were right. You know it when you see it, and you cannot lead without it. You also cannot sleep at night, look yourself in the mirror, or die happy without it.

The closest I can come to a definition of integrity is authenticity, or "being yourself." If you are not genuine with others or yourself, you will almost always lead them into a bad place. If you lead with integrity and are authentic about it, you may not always get to the "right" place, but you will have solid relationships, legitimate purpose, and a good life both professionally and personally.

When you have integrity, you can also admit mistakes and accept forgiveness, you can forgive others, you can move on in uncertainty and freedom rather than seeking a false security based in fear. You do not let the perfect ruin the good. This is a tough way to be in corporate America, but bypassing the drama for authentic interaction is good business and real leadership.

Warning: It will, however, often scare the hell out of people.

Part I

A New Way of Thinking

Relationships Matter

WHY *A GUIDE TO LEADERSHIP AND MANAGEMENT IN HIGHER EDUCATION: MANAGING ACROSS THE GENERATIONS?*

For the first time in contemporary history, four generations of employees work side by side, bringing to the workplace their own unique set of talents, needs and expectations (Toossi, 2012). A natural extension of this phenomenon is a change to the workplace itself, as each generation brings its own set of values, priorities and work styles. Keeping pace with these changes, while maintaining our sea legs against the changing tides of higher education, will be the focus of this book.

Leadership within higher education takes a divergent path from business leadership. We are, after all, educators at heart. We hold a belief in the transformational power of education. We lead our students by being. However, when the lens turns from our students to our staff, a shift happens. The technical skills of management begin to matter more than ever before and, while we may be educators at heart, the business of education is an arena where we may find ourselves unprepared.

The exploration of leadership across generations comes amid a changing paradigm in higher education. The current model is one of increased focus on outcomes. And, while the pursuit of results and metrics measuring factors of effectiveness for a successful college or university is laudable, an over-reliance on contemporary cognitive, solution-driven management approaches in a higher education setting can be seen as a case of square peg/round hole.

So, why read this book? You want to be a better leader in order to increase the effectiveness of your department? You need to positively impact student retention? You wish to get the most out of your staff in order to operate leaner? You imagine seeing your staff use their strengths and soar? Some or all of the above? Keep reading.

A CHANGING AGE

Let us begin by exploring what is, for many, the current narrative in leadership: A cognitive, solution-focused approach, but which may not be effective in leadership of a cross-generational workforce. Why? In his work, *A Whole New Mind: Why Right-brainers Will Rule the Future* (2005), Daniel Pink explores the shifting tide from left- to right-brained approaches by presenting the reader with an overview of the four major ages. He describes the current movement from the most recent Information Age, characterized by *knowledge workers*, and introduces the current Conceptual Age, characterized by *empathy and creativity*. Pink posits that leaders who focus on creativity and innovation will be the successful leaders of the future. What is so resonant about this assertion is its relationship to the generations in confluence with this new age: Generation X and Millennials, characterized by their empathy and creative innovation respectively.

Cognitive, solution-focused leadership approaches were developed to be responsive to the needs of a left brain focused workforce during a time of rapid technological change for knowledge-focused workforce management. Taking a cue from Pink's work, we acknowledge that a changing age calls for new ways of leadership. Pink's work urges an understanding of the contemporary Conceptual Age and presents leaders within the realm of higher education with an opportunity to shift the way we interact with *staff*, more closely aligning this to the way we have traditionally interacted with our *students*.

Indeed, even traditional business is changing. Starbucks CEO Howard Schultz is famously quoted as saying, "Care more than others think wise." At Google, Chade-Meng Tan developed *Search Inside Yourself*, a program he describes as "the unexpected path to achieving success, happiness (and world peace)." This program, and the book of the same name (Tan, 2012), provide a case study in the application of mindfulness meditation as a means to increase emotional intelligence, and of compassion and self-knowledge as building blocks to success in business and in life.

Four Letter Words Go To Work: Love, Care, and Hope

In his book, *Love is the Killer App: How to Win Business and Influence Friends* (2002), Tim Sanders, Chief Solutions Officer for Yahoo, explores the application of love in business; he calls this approach being a "Lovecat," and he is convinced that this is the way to be a success in business and to make friends. Sanders isn't alone; Princeton Business Professor Robert Sutton explores the concepts of care and civility in his book, *The No Asshole Rule: Building a Civilized Workplace and Surviving One That Isn't* (2007). Most recently, in his book, *Making Hope Happen: Create the Future You Want for Yourself and Others* (2014), Shane Lopez explores hope as a human emotion and helps the reader understand the power of hope to effect change.

Why are so many thought leaders writing about love, care and hope? And, what does this mean to higher education leaders and their staff who are responsible for stewarding young people into adulthood and who must adapt to the changing tide of each new generation? In order to stay relevant and effective, higher education leadership must evolve to meet the conditions in which it exists. While we might have always *cared for, and even loved our staff*, the time to begin authentic leadership relationships with these particular four letter words squarely at its foundation, is now.

Barriers to Change

As leaders, we hold a particular privilege, and as with any position of privilege, it is a foundational task to recognize and acknowledge this privilege so that we can think, act, and (most importantly) feel differently (Malcolm, 2005). However, to care is to make oneself vulnerable, and this may be a primary barrier to shifting ways of looking at leadership. It isn't that we propose an obligation to behave a certain way; rather, that

5

vulnerability with employees accomplishes two things: First, it suggests that supervisors adopt a stance of reflection and humility that allows for deeper insight and creates opportunities to build connection and trust with their employees—people tend to follow and seek guidance from those that they trust, and can sense a quality of genuineness and congruence in word and in deed. Second, by acknowledging the privilege of leadership and carrying it softly and with grace, leaders provide employees with a model of behavior to emulate with students.

Relationships and communication should become the *lingua franca* of the office, providing opportunities to better understand the motivations of employees to improve efficiency and effectiveness on tasks. In a world dominated by 360-degree evaluations and annual performance appraisals, there is the real potential of losing track of the individual humanity of our staff and the needs of those struggling to find a larger sense of meaning and purpose in the workplace. By attending to these underlying needs, managers and supervisors can better motivate and inspire staff to focus on work-related tasks. Ignoring these underlying needs leads to a disengaged workforce resulting in excessive use of sick days, lack of productivity, and employees who are working—in the words of Peter Gibbons from the movie *Office Space*—"just hard enough to not get fired." (Sound like anyone you know?)

It is this authentic, genuine, personal caring that becomes the gasoline in the tank that helps improve productivity and effectiveness of the employee. We all work harder for a supervisor who cares about us as people. By connecting to this deeper well of personhood, the manager unlocks the potential of the employee and becomes the standard by which future opportunities and challenges are addressed.

ACROSS GENERATIONS

A natural intersection of this shift in focus on an authentic relational dynamic in the management and supervision process, is attention to the generational differences and conflicts that exist in the changing workplace. These exist as potential hotspots, but also as opportunities for growth among co-workers, managers and leaders, as the four generations—Millennials, Gen Xer's, Boomers and Matures—interact and must collaborate and cooperate with each other, in order to foster a productive workplace.

The disconnect between current leadership styles and the college and university workforce is particularly startling to our Millennial staff, having only just transitioned from the warm embrace of their own studies. Indeed, the question "What do Millennials want?" within the context of the workplace is the *question du jour* for many leaders.

But in our zest to understand the newest, and now largest, proportion of the workforce, let us not forget the Gen Xer's who are simultaneously graduating their children from high school while caring for aging parents (Fry, 2015). Boomers are looking toward (delayed) retirement while caring for their aging parents. Matures have likewise maintained their employment and delayed retirement in direct response to the shrinking retirement accounts resulting from the Great Recession.

Imagine a scenario where Sara, a Millennial staff member, is being supervised by a Boomer named Karl. The supervisor struggles to understand why the younger staff member lacks attention to detail and seems to have a poor work ethic in terms of completing tasks on time and showing initiative on projects. Sara sees Karl as out of touch with current technology and social media and as unwilling to be flexible on project timelines and daily expectations around customer service. Conversations between the two are unproductive and often dissolve into Karl feeling like Sara just needs to buckle down and get things done. Sara has little faith in Karl's leadership and decision-making and feels that no matter what she does, it won't meet Karl's standards.

Leaders and managers who excel in the higher education workplace do so through an awareness of the challenges faced by each of the four generations as they interact with each other and with their students. While it would be over-expansive to suggest that all of the challenges in the workplace center on these generational differences—addressing the differences in worldview—communication style and motivation is one important step toward improving productivity and building a balanced and efficient team. In the case of Karl and Sara, the challenge becomes helping each understand the potentially limiting ways they see each other and how to establish a common ground that allows for an appreciation of the contributions of one another within the workplace, fostering better communication and observable progress.

Never has it been more critical for leaders to create an environment of mutual understanding and authentic care for their teams. The unprecedented intersection of four generations of employees in the contemporary workplace presents an opportunity for leaders within higher education to capitalize on the diverse strengths and expertise of their workforce, and to demonstrate a willingness to understand and meet their employees' priorities and work styles. This opportunity comes at a time of critical change in higher education, and may well be the answer to running leaner and more productive teams.

EXAMPLE FROM THE EXPERT—
1.1: LESSONS LEARNED AS A MILLENNIAL MANAGER

Being a supervisor is an often misunderstood role. I grew up "understanding" the corporate world to a certain extent from my father—the CFO of a few large technology companies in Silicon Valley. From my vantage point, I expected that as a boss you get cool perks, go out to fancy dinners and buy nice cars. As the boss, you make all of the decisions and hold all of the power. As a boss, you know everything and are respected for it. Not a bad gig!

It wasn't until I got my first job that I realized I truly had no idea what my dad did as an executive, and that I actually had no idea what it took to be a supervisor. What I assumed from the stereotypical management roles played on television, and what I vaguely knew of my dad ended up being contradictory to what I experienced when I entered the world of higher education.

Only a year after starting my first real job out of college, at just 23-years-old, I was promoted to a manager of actual people, most of whom were older than me. As is sometimes the case, this promotion occurred not because I had managerial experience, but because I was very good at my job. Talk about a steep learning curve!

Let me be honest, back then, I was really only concerned about myself, with few obligations in life and a bright future ahead. All I thought was: *Here come the perks, the ability to make big decisions and getting respect for being the smartest person in the room!* That's not exactly how it went, so let me share a bit of what I learned in those very early years leading a diverse, cross-generational team.

You get a great deal of ~~perks~~ responsibility when you become a manager

What I quickly discovered in my first year as a new (read: naïve) Millennial manager, is that I had a great responsibility to the people I supervised who worked for more than just themselves. I've often heard the phrase, "leave your personal life at the door" and regretfully, I've seen people treat their staff with this attitude. But as I got to know my team on a deeper level, particularly those who were farther along in life than I was, I found that their personal lives were what kept them motivated to come to work and to work hard each day; in fact, it was their personal lives that gave them a reason to keep going!

And if something happened to their job, their personal life would suffer—their children, their goals, their plans; it would all suffer.

That's when I realized that I played a huge role in the personal lives of my staff by being responsible for their professional lives. As a manager, I discovered that it was my responsibility to value and challenge and encourage my team, and to do whatever it took to help them to succeed, because if they failed it would impact them far beyond the office walls. Unfortunately, I've seen far too many young managers forget this fact, focusing on the "perks" rather than the people. *If all managers understood the seriousness of the responsibility they take on when becoming a supervisor, I truly believe that there would be a major improvement in overall employee engagement and success.*

You get to make important decisions—together

I also learned that one person can't make decisions. Actually, let me rephrase: It's powerful to think that one person has the ability to make changes and choices for all, but only self-important managers actually do. I've very clearly found that when you bring people together to be part of the decision-making process, trust is established and buy-in is created. It doesn't mean that the popular vote dictates the outcome, it simply means that there is a collaboration process that occurs to come to the decision. This process takes additional time, but it also ensures that as a manager one is taking into account the widest possible aspects of a situation, with transparency being at the forefront. *Call this Millennial thinking, but I've found that a work culture that fosters the sharing of thoughts and the challenging of ideas has been embraced by employees of all ages.*

You *earn* respect by *giving* respect—to the real experts

When I first became a manager, I thought that I was expected to be the smartest person in every area of our jobs. Of course, that's impossible, but I was terrified that my team would find out about my "weaknesses" and ultimately lose respect for me as their leader. It took some time letting down my guard to find out that it wasn't important for me to know everything, but it *was* important to recognize those who were experts in certain areas and call on them to be leaders. I had a team of competent, tenured, accomplished people

9

who each had expertise in different areas. It went a long way—especially with the more senior members—for me to be honest with what I knew and didn't know, recognize their skills, allow them to be the experts, and to be OK with asking them for help when needed. *In the end, realizing that respect is a two-way street is what ultimately earned respect from my team.*

Aimee Slade, M.A.
Associate Director of Quality Assurance, Office of the Registrar
Ashford University

EXAMPLE FROM THE EXPERT—
1.2: RESPECT AND SUPPORT—WHAT WE ALL NEED TO BE SUCCESSFUL

In my office, I have a framed quote by Clarence Darrow: "Lost causes are the only ones worth fighting for." I have always drawn inspiration from the sentiment Darrow perfectly captures in such a succinct manner, although in reality I can honestly say I have never actually met a "lost cause."

As anyone who spends any time in academia comes to realize fairly quickly, higher education is one of the more political careers one can choose to pursue. This is true regardless of whether you are on the "faculty" or the "staff" side of the aisle. True, the nature of the political games differ somewhat, but at their core they represent the same struggle for power, recognition, acceptance and credibility that inevitably develops when people with varying degrees of insecurity share the same work environment.

A few years ago a colleague of mine who worked in administration was overlooked for a key promotion. This person, who we will call "Molly," was eminently qualified for the position she was ultimately unsuccessful in attaining, but the problem was she was not in the inner circle of the senior administrator—who had the ultimate decision-making authority over the selection process.

Molly was competent, intelligent, organized and motivated; moreover, she had excellent people skills and an unshakable desire to do the proverbial "right thing"—especially when it came to serving students. As is often the case, however, this made her a threat to her less qualified colleagues. For the less capable, it is always easier to try and pull others down to your level than to put forth the effort needed to raise yourself to a higher plane.

As a consequence of the politics involved in the search process, which became quite ugly before it was all over, Molly was eventually reassigned to my department as a junior faculty member—which was perfectly all right with me as I had tried to get her to apply for a faculty position in my program pretty much since she first arrived at our institution.

Up to this point, I had never really seen myself as a mentor; certainly not in any formal sense. In fact, I still saw myself as *needing* mentors rather than *being* one. But it quickly became apparent Molly needed someone to empathize with her plight and to appreciate her for the talented person she was—and still is. Having spent some time as a mid-level administrator, I could relate to what she had gone through and I was determined to make her transition to faculty as tranquil as possible.

At first, Molly wasn't sure she could trust me, which is understandable. Anyone who had just been through what she had experienced would no doubt be a little hesitant to take anything at face value. After all, I had once worked closely with several of the staff members who were threatened (although they would never admit it) by her tremendous ability and expertise.

I started off by simply offering to help her get acclimated to the department and especially to her new colleagues. I offered advice on how best to negotiate the new kind of politics she now found herself submerged within. As we all know, human beings would be lost without pecking orders, and assistant professors (Molly's new position) are on the low end of the continuum when it comes to academia. Slowly but surely, as she sensed my sincerity in wanting her to be successful, she began to develop into the tremendously effective educator that she was always capable of becoming.

To be honest, Molly was a godsend. I had been the only full-time faculty member assigned to my program for some years so it was nice to actually have a true colleague. Within a short period of time, we were engaged in some writing projects, submitting proposals to several professional conferences, and revising the curriculum of the graduate program in which we taught. It was nice to have someone who shared my enthusiasm for developing students to their maximumpotential; someone who shared my belief that preparing the next generation of dedicated professionals was indeed a noble calling.

I learned from working with Molly that what most of us need early in our careers is simply the support and respect of our senior colleagues—that is, those in leadership roles above us on the organizational chart. We need to feel our contributions are meaningful and that we do indeed have something valuable to offer. We need to be appreciated for our talents, not penalized for them or held in suspicion. All Molly needed was the right environment and the sky was the limit.

Molly has since earned tenure, been promoted, and will probably be my department head at some point—which is fine with me. The small part I played in helping her to realize the potential she had long before she met me is a reward in itself. I got into education because I believe all most of us need to be successful in work and in life is for someone to believe in us and support us as we progress on our journey.

The more I reflect on Clarence Darrow's quote, the more I feel he was on to something profound. In the final analysis, there are no "lost causes"—there are only those who make others feel they are. Everyone needs the opportunity to demonstrate what they are truly capable of, and providing the opportunity for them to do so is one of the most consequential roles any leader can assume.

Aaron W. Hughey, Ed.D.
Professor and Program Coordinator,
Department of Counseling and Student Affairs
Western Kentucky University

It is our hope that this book provides you, the reader, with novel, inspiring and even challenging information to assist you in reflecting on your management and leadership style within the context of generational diversity. Even more than understanding the differences inherent in the four generations that comprise today's workforce, however, is the essential focus on our similarities and the desire for all employees to find meaning in their work and to feel cared about and valued. We will offer a review of theories from leaders in the field, and practical examples from those who have been doing this work for decades. It is our desire that this book brings together our common goals to create a caring, productive and successful workplace—and hence, workforce.

EXAMPLE FROM THE EXPERT—
1.3: BUILDING RELATIONSHIPS IS ESSENTIAL TO LEADERSHIP

I have always lived by the saying "It's not who you know, it's who knows you."

Understanding this concept fully will help you not only in landing leadership positions, but in keeping them as well. Focusing on who knows you will earn you the respect of your superiors, colleagues, clients, students, and your staff. Who really knows you? Who knows what you bring to the table? Who have you worked with closely on major accomplishments? Or if you worked alone, who did you tell about your accomplishments? Did you toot your own horn? If not, you must! If people haven't had the opportunity to work with you collaboratively, they really cannot serve as a useful reference and will not think of you when appropriate opportunities arise.

If you do not regularly share what you are doing, people will wrongly assume that you are doing nothing. Without documenting the planning, energy, and effort that you contribute to your organization's successes, things may wrongly appear to just function magically. So, build relationships, seek partnerships, explore opportunities with others so they really get to know you, your authentic self, and all of the leadership gifts you and your team bring to the table. Follow up by showing accountability for your actions and spread the word about your impact and successes. By doing this you are modeling for others, and your positive energy will radiate throughout your organization.

Building relationships is essential to leadership.

Adrienne C. Brown
Career Center Director, UMOJA Director/Counselor
Los Angeles Harbor College

DISCUSSION QUESTIONS

1. How do you see generational differences impacting the way leaders, supervisors and managers do their work?

2. In your opinion, is there room for love, care and hope in the workplace? What are some of the benefits in approaching leadership and managing with a focus on these viewpoints? What are some of the challenges or obstacles to using terms like "love," "care" and "hope" in the workplace?

3. What are some of the specific challenges you have encountered in managing or leading those from the Millennial generation? What messages do our society and the media portray when considering Millennials in the workplace? In your experience, are these portrayals accurate or inaccurate?

4. What are some challenges that you see for leaders and managers in today's workplace that are different from challenges faced by previous generations? What are some ways to overcome these obstacles?

5. The authors introduce "Examples from the Experts" to help demonstrate practical experiences of leaders and managers in the field of higher education. Give an example of where you have had a positive experience with a director, department head or supervisor in your work experience? What qualities do you look for in a manager or leader?

Just One Thing

Josh E. Gunn, Ph.D.
Executive Director, Counseling and Psychological Services
Kennesaw State University

The two primary components of any work are tasks and relationships. I've found in leadership, the more time-consuming yet fruitful of these two components is relationships. Leadership for me is the constant attending to, negotiating and renegotiating of relationships. And relationships are two-way streets. Leadership is not only having awareness of those being supervised; rather, leaders must also be intensely self-aware if they are going to have the interpersonal impact that makes folks want to follow. Additionally, leadership inherently involves legitimate authority; the secret to leading well seems to be using various types of authority—and then only as much as needed—to complete the task at hand while enhancing or minimizing impact on relationships.

Chapter Two

Exploring Generational Diversity
Surrender the Cliché

> **KEY TAKE-A-WAYS**
>
> ■ In a time of unprecedented multi-generational diversity, it is critical to creating and maintaining a successful higher education workplace that leaders and managers attend to this element of workforce diversity.
> ■ The success of departments, units or divisions depends largely on the ability of leaders and managers to establish cohesive teams across a multitude of diverse boundaries, to demonstrate and foster supportive and respectful relationships, and to establish shared goals and vision for their teams.
> ■ Leaders and managers must examine competing concepts while embracing a willingness to surrender those clichés that act as a barrier to capitalizing on the talents of all team members, while investing time to build an understanding of the current generations from a 20,000 foot view in order to understand their values, priorities and work styles.

The American workforce finds itself in a time of unprecedented multi-generational diversity. For the first time, four generations of workers collaborate in the conference room, and commingle in the break room. This richness of diversity can be traced to a rising retirement age resulting from the Great Recession, a need to retain an aging skilled workforce, and an influx of *new-to-the-work-world Millennials.* But, is generational diversity meaningful in a contemporary higher education workplace?

At the door of higher education leaders and managers, the current four-generation span has arrived, and with it, their unique work styles, attitudes and priorities, requiring attention. Leaders and managers are charged with understanding and effectively interacting with a richly diverse workforce that includes diversity of race, ethnicity, gender, gender identity, sexual orientation, ability, and generational diversity, which will be the focus of this chapter. The success of their departments, units or divisions depends largely on the ability of leaders and managers to establish cohesive teams across a multitude of these diverse boundaries, to demonstrate and foster supportive and respectful relationships, and to establish shared goals and vision for their teams. In his work, *The Speed of Trust: The one thing that changes everything* (2006), Stephen M. R. Covey built an entire workplace philosophy predicated upon trust as a critical factor for success, and understanding as a building block of trust.

UNDERSTANDING GENERATIONS

A generation can be defined as the aggregate of all people born over a span of roughly twenty years. Pioneers in our modern understanding of generations, Strauss and Howe's work in *The Fourth Turning* (1997) moves us beyond this static definition, to weave in intersections of place, time and age (or development) as a more accurate way to describe the generational phenomenon. They describe a generation as being comprised of the twenty-year span, plus the commonalities of developmental stage (childhood or early adulthood) and *location in history* (historical events and social trends). This shared developmental/historical experience tends to produce a similarity of *common beliefs and behaviors* (in the workplace, this may be seen as work styles, attitudes and priorities). Owing to an awareness of these common beliefs and behaviors, members of a given generation are said to have a *common perceived membership* in that generation.

A most effective way to demonstrate this phenomenon is to ask members of a specific generation about a historical event that occurred during their childhood or early adulthood. For example, ask a Boomer for their account of the day that John F. Kennedy was assassinated or of Martin Luther King Jr.'s march on Washington, or ask a Gen Xer for their account of the events of 9/11 or the slow-speed pursuit of O.J. Simpson. Demonstrated in this exercise, one sees that it is the combination of *developmental place in time* layered atop *historical context* that produces the rich and varied tapestry of the generation.

It's All About Me (Millennials)

As we begin this discussion, let us address the elephant in the room. You may, in fact, be reading this book in order to better understand the

Millennials in your division or department. In undertaking a discussion of generational diversity, we wish to address directly the topic of Millennials, the special snowflakes you have come to love, and the "helicopter parents" who have emerged, not coincidentally, during our work with Millennials as students. Colloquially, the term describes those parents who are overprotective and potentially stunting to the growth and development of their children. The relationship between Millennial child and parent is, in fact, a defining characteristic of this generation which we will explore more fully later in this chapter.

It is our view that the famously infamous stories we tell over water-coolers are representative of a perfect storm of outlier parents. These folks, acting in downright ridiculous ways—calling their kids ten times a day, doing their laundry for them in the basement of the dorm, reading and editing assignments and papers, or yelling at housing staff to provide better accommodations for their child—coalesce against our collective frustration. We observe parents coddling their children, most notably evidenced in the now famous "participation ribbons" that hang ubiquitously in every Millennial's childhood bedroom. *And then, after all of that, we are meant to employ the children of these parents!*

At worst, Millennials are described as lazy, unmotivated and lacking initiative to complete assignments and work tasks. As with helicopter parents, the argument we make here is that this perception—exemplified by the extreme, not the mean—coincides with our collective frustration around this newest to the workplace generation. We argue that we are the proverbial grandparent throwing up hands and exclaiming, "*In my day, we walked to school five miles in the snow, uphill both ways!*" (Stay with us!) We challenge our reader to consider the perceived lack of work ethic and the resulting clichés which are unproductive and serve only to foster damaging stereotypes of this newest, and now largest, generation in the workforce (Table 2.1).

EXPLORING THE FOUR GENERATIONS

Generations are like people. At a macro level they have unique personalities and stories. As leaders, the better our understanding of the generations, the more effectively we capitalize on the talents and contributions of all our staff.

The contemporary workforce includes Matures (also, the Silent Generation), known most commonly as company men; Baby Boomers, a generation of civil activists and the echo effect of post-war era prosperity; Generation X, by the numbers a smaller and gentler generation whose focus on human rights and equity define them; and finally, Millennials

Table 2.1 Overview of the Generations and % of the Total Workforce

Generation	Born	Members in Workforce	% of Total Workforce
Matures (also, Silent Generation)	1925–1942	3.7M	2%
Baby Boomers	1943–1960	44.6M	29%
Generation X	1961–1981	52.7M	34%
Millennials (also, Gen Y)	1982–2004	53.5M	35%

Source: Fry, R. (2015), Pew Research Center

(also Gen Y), commonly referenced as the "me generation" and an echo of the prosperity of the 80s and 90s—now the largest living generation, and as of 2015, the largest overall proportion of today's workforce.

The changes in these generations include a soon-to-be majority non-white population and record graying, or increases in life expectancy, and these shifts are creating unprecedented generation gaps that have the potential to result in a lack of social cohesion, particularly in the workplace (Fry, 2015).

Matures (also, the Silent Generation)

Matures, now only 2% of the total workforce, are the most seasoned generation and are likely to effect their impact as high-level leaders on college and university campuses. They are conservative rule-followers who have lived through wars and seen waves of social change unfold through activism, civil unrest, and the turning tides of time. Matures are the least diverse generation as eight in ten are white (Fry, 2015). Matures understand that everything old is new again and bring with them a sage wisdom informed by age and experience. To younger generations, they may be seen as being out of touch with a fast-moving, technology-enabled workplace.

Leaders and managers may risk not capitalizing on the talents of Matures as their numbers dwindle and they move toward retirement.

Boomers (also, Baby Boomers)

Boomers, now 29% of the total workforce, are the largest seasoned generation and effect their impact as mid- and high-level leaders on college and university campuses. Boomers may have delayed retirement, remaining in the workforce in direct response to shrinking retirement accounts resulting from the Great Recession, combined with the uncomfortable sandwich

19

between caring for children at home, and caring for their aging, longer living parents. Boomers were counter-cultural civil activists whose blood, sweat and tears manifested the Civil Rights Act, bore the women's liberation movement and protested the Vietnam War. Owing to their counterculture youth, Boomers may be the oldest relatable generation to employees, often being well liked and inspirational in their leadership abilities.

Leaders and managers may find themselves struggling to honor the historical position of Boomers in the workplace, given they have long enjoyed a position of power and attention there—that may wane as Generation X and Millennials come forward with new ideas, energy and technological savvy.

Generation X (also, Gen X)

Generation X, only recently unseated by Millennials as the largest overall proportion of the contemporary workforce, make up 34% of workers and are seen as having big dreams and big hearts. These savvy, cynical problem-solvers are liberals who lean left. In youth, they coined the phrase "mean people suck." Latchkey kids of high divorce rates—raised on Mr Rogers and Sesame Street—those in Generation X often find themselves in need of praise and feedback. A swan song for the generation, Kurt Cobain's 1991 "Smells Like Teen Spirit" lyric, *Here we are now, entertain us* characterized Gen X, as did Winona Ryder's *Reality Bites.* Gen Xer's are the rising tide of young leaders and are effective in this role, often working well at inspiring others to tasks.

Leaders and managers may risk not capitalizing on Gen Xer's if they do not secure their buy-in prior to asking for their support, as Gen Xer's typically have an aversion to the status quo, rejecting simply doing things because they are told to do so.

Millennials (also, Gen Y)

Millennials range in age from mid-teens to early 30s, make up 35% and are the largest overall proportion of the workforce. In youth, Millennials have evidenced lower rates of teen suicide, pregnancy and abortion, and violent crime and drug use. These digital natives are the most diverse generation; about half are non-white. They are slow to get jobs, buy homes and marry; having begun their economic lives during the Great Recession, they experienced a lack of economic foundation. Nevertheless, Millennials are optimists.

The Millennials' focus on teamwork positions them well to be future leaders, once professional experience and gravitas can be added to their resumes. Leaders and managers may risk not capitalizing on Millennial staff by presuming short attention spans and even shorter tenure within organizations. Strauss and Howe suggest that no other adult group possesses their team player, high achieving reputation (2003). And, it is against this description that the clichéd "Millennial as lazy and unmotivated" is most concerning. What is true of the Millennial is their determination to work *and* play in ways that previous generations could never have imagined.

Finally, back to those helicopter parents; technology-enabled relationships mean that parents of Millennials had more—and more immediate—access to information about their children. These parental relationships are characterized by interdependency, which may be seen as problematic both in Millennials as students and as employees. Ultimately, this is the context in which they have emerged, and we do well to recognize that Millennials have as little control over the behavior of their helicopter parents as we do!

TRANSCENDING CLICHÉ

For leaders and managers, this role requires that we move beyond the clichéd views of specific generations—e.g., *Millennials as the "me" generation*—in order to increase understanding and build solid foundations for relational trust and workplace success. To do so requires the holding of competing concepts: first, we must embrace a willingness to surrender those damaging stereotypes that act as a barrier to capitalizing on the talents of all team members. This means an investment in knowing our teams rather than making suppositions about them based upon generational stereotypes; this means acknowledging that all Millennials are not lazy, because, of course, we know that is not true. Conversely, we simultaneously invest in increasing our understanding of generations from a 20,000 foot view, free from cliché, but with an acknowledgement of the abiding truth of generational characteristics, priorities and values.

Looking to popular culture, these stereotypes are interestingly inflated in Noah Baumbach's 2015 film, *While We're Young*, starring Ben Stiller as a forty-something Gen Xer, and his new Gen Y friend, played by Adam Driver. The film tells the story of Josh (Stiller), a documentary film-maker and his semi-protégé Jamie (Driver). The generational cliché of Millennials as lazy, entitled narcissists with an affinity for nostalgia and ironic t-shirts, and of Gen Xer's as now middle-aged discontents does little to address the generational dynamics between the two men (and more broadly, between the two generations). It is, unfortunately, well played and entertaining, and thus propagates the very clichés of which we speak. (*See* the film, just don't *buy* it.)

In our first *Example from the Expert*, David J. Denino, Director Emeritus, Counseling Services at Southern Connecticut State University,

21

explores some ways that leaders and managers can find success in capitalizing on their Millennials' talent. To summarize this list, Millennials (and perhaps the rest of your workforce!) will benefit from the three Cs: Collaboration, Communication and Care. (There's that four letter word again!)

EXAMPLE FROM THE EXPERT—
2.1: ACROSS GENERATIONS—MILLENNIALS

She walks into the interview with great surety that the job is hers. Isabelle earned her first sports awards before kindergarten and the trophies and medals became too numerous to count. Everyone wins, all of the time. Always encouraged to be anything she wants to be, and she has basked in the positive attention and praise given by her Boomer parents. First of many I would encounter either working as an administrator or as an adjunct professor.

Time magazine released an article titled "Millennials: the Me Me Me Generation", which called Gen Y's lazy, entitled, self-obsessed narcissists. However, they also qualify as being open-minded, liberal, self-expressive, upbeat, and overtly passionate about equality. In between lies the balance of what Isabelle will become as an adult and what will make meaning for her and those around her.

Back to that interview and working in a higher education setting. What makes Isabelle so different than the students that preceded her that I've interviewed and worked with in the 70s, 80s and 90s? Drive, confidence, entitlement, self-expressive, liberal, upbeat and receptive to new ideas and ways of living are some traits; those are muddled with *Time* magazine's noting they're lazy, narcissistic, coddled, and maybe even a bit delusional.

The task for managing this conundrum in higher education is to know the values of each of the generations that we work with in the office or the classroom. I'm acknowledging that having close to a forty-year career in higher education as an administrator, counselor and part-time professor, it felt sometimes like a struggle I did not need to have. Why can't new generations just simply have the work ethic that we Boomers had? Well, change is a higher education principle, and I often recalled Bill Clinton's campaign messages, "It's the economy, stupid" along with "change vs. more of the same," as precipitating factors for this new generation. With that, it was indeed the new generation and change needed to be embraced.

Isabelle and her accolade champions cohort needed to be embraced yet not coddled. Since there does seem to be more of an emphasis on the self than in previous generations, how do we embrace and not coddle? That's been both challenging and successful for me so I am pleased to suggest some uncomplicated ways in which you can have success by embracing Millennial talent.

1. They are multitaskers! Absolutely can handle lots at once, but often you will find texting and social media infiltrating. So it's important to establish your expectations in the office/classroom with daily/weekly goals.
2. Take an interest in their success. They are achievement oriented. So give them opportunities for measurable achievements and advancement, with concrete targets. Keys can be to provide an empathic setting that is equal to accountability.
3. Plan to be collaborative. They are extremely team-oriented and enjoy collaborating and building friendships with colleagues. Allow them to work in groups when possible.
4. Communicate—a lot! That accolade champion cohort grew up inside a supportive environment in which they were told they WILL achieve, irrespective of the facts. So, immediate feedback becomes important, and we must accept it and work it for positive outcomes. Provide advice, criticism, appreciation, and guidance in the moment.
5. Offer formal mentoring. Isabelle and her cohort are extremely teachable and receptive to formal mentoring. Keep it simple too—by giving training in your office protocols or expectations in the classroom. After all, behavior is a learned experience.
6. Be willing to meet in the middle. In my four decades of higher ed work, I have marched through with the Boomers (*my* cohort!), Xer's, Yer's/Millennials, and Zer's. Through all that, my best piece of advice is this: Be open to your own frailties and misgivings. Learn about them as they learn about you and you'll find solid middle ground.

With reference to the last item, intergenerational conflicts can become commonplace. The beliefs that each generation hold can lead to conflict, making "other" people harder to understand. With that, it's important to know that Millennials work best with clear guidelines, frequent and immediate feedback, solid perspective, clarity and independence. Their preferences are to work in teams and make group decisions that can be considered and achieved. Not having to deal with ambiguity and slow processes is a factor (think social media formats) and they do indeed value trust and transparency.

Change vs. more of the same. Isabelle and her friends got the job, and we all expanded our horizons.

David J. Denino
Director Emeritus, Counseling Services
Southern Connecticut State University

GENERATIONAL VALUES IN CONFLICT

Cesar and Lisa

Cesar is a Boomer and Director of Library Services for a small University. He has been with the University for nearly 25 years and is ready for retirement. He is grateful for the stability and meaning his job has provided to him. Cesar has been loyal to the University and worked his way up through the ranks to his current position. One of the primary concerns that Cesar has about retirement is that he doesn't see an adequate fit for his replacement within the ranks of the Library staff.

Lisa is a junior Librarian who first worked as an intern while pursuing her Masters at the University. She is a Gen Xer who returned to school in her thirties to pursue her passion for Library Science, frequently discusses other job opportunities, and has shared openly with Cesar when she has applied for other positions that she sees as opportunities to move up.

While Cesar sees Lisa as highly capable and appreciates that she has some professional experience from her prior career to add to the skillset she brings to the University, her lack of loyalty and willingness to pay her dues is frustrating to Cesar. He worries that if he retires, and Lisa was selected to replace him, the Library would suffer if she were to leave after a year or two.

Lisa struggles to connect to Cesar. She notices that he bristles when she talks about career progression and seeks his mentorship on the topic. Lisa values Cesar's professional experience, but she can't seem to get the support she needs from him. To Lisa, having already gone back to school to make a career shift, professional progression is one of the most important priorities she has identified for the next five years; she is willing to leave her current institution, and even to relocate, if it means she will be able to progress in her career. To Cesar, Lisa's apparent lack of loyalty prevents him from making the investment in her development, necessary for her to be able to take on a more responsible role.

The values and differences that they bring to the table present a typical generational workplace conflict that prevents both Cesar and Lisa from having their needs met. Cesar is looking forward to retirement, but is reluctant to leave his Library without the leadership he believes it deserves. Lisa is capable, and looking forward to a more responsible career progression, but because she is so open about this, Cesar judges her to be lacking in loyalty and a willingness to pay her dues.

Lisa, as a Gen Xer, grew up in the post-pension era. Corporate loyalty and staying power were never a part of Lisa's worldview, standing in stark contrast to Cesar's generational and lived experiences of stability and loyalty. The irony of this example, of course, is that Cesar and Lisa want the same things, but their differences prevent them from recognizing that they can find them in one another!

ANTICIPATING AND UNDERSTANDING CONFLICT

It isn't enough to learn about our generational differences, we must better understand the potential for those differences to turn into harmful generational stereotypes. This occurs when differences in values emerge as conflict within the workplace (also, in any house where a teenager and their parents cohabit). Recognizing that our values are the bedrock of who we are, we can see the potential for conflict that can emerge when values differ. Add heat to these generational-based conflicts when one generation supervises, and therefore has power over, the other. Understanding the generational differences that exist across the workforce and the potential for conflicts that arise out of these differences is a leadership skill critical to anticipating and addressing them.

EXAMPLE FROM THE EXPERT—
2.2: REFLECTIONS OF A MILLENNIAL ON SUPERVISION STYLES

Similar to many, I began working in the field of student affairs prior to realizing, as an undergraduate and extremely involved student, that the field existed. The field's appeal to me began when I first walked on campus at Mount Union College in Alliance, Ohio when I met my admissions tour guide and counselor who seemed genuinely excited to meet and show me around campus. Fast-forward a few months, I met my "Preview and Orientation Guides" who appeared to have an extremely fun job as they led our group through "games," which I quickly learned had the purpose of introducing us to each other and the campus. When I returned in the fall a few days before class began, said goodbye to my parents and boyfriend who dropped me off, I felt sad and alone for only a short amount of time before I walked onto the quad and was met by approximately 650 other students who were inevitably feeling similar.

It was only a few days later that I met who would be my first supervisor, the Director of Student Involvement & Leadership. He was also the first person to deny me a job for the first time. I applied to be a Preview and Orientation Guide during the fall of my first year on campus and because I was not involved in other programs or activities, I was told this was not the way to jumpstart my involvement. I was devastated but took the feedback as a challenge to curb both my homesickness and do just the thing that had kept me from being hired for the first job I truly wanted in my life. I involved myself in my academic major and in the programming board during the next year and was able to communicate the way my involvement assisted in my transition to college. It was during my sophomore year that I applied again for the same post and was hired for the summer leading up to my junior year. During that year, through my academic department, I also got further involved in the programming board and in organizations. It was also then that my first supervisor informed me that I could do this as a living. I, again like many of us, said, "do what as a living?" Which is also when I learned about the field of student affairs through this same supervisor, who was born into Generation X. I tell this story because it informed my very first expectations of a supervisor and ways in which I wish to supervise professionals, graduate assistants, and highly involved student leaders. It is a combination of the ability to deny someone who is not ready for a new initiative or project, push them to do more when necessary, and celebrate with them when they have achieved their goals.

I have primarily had supervisors from Generation X who have shown me the ways in which I wanted and needed to be supervised. I often reflect on their styles when I write or answer the questions of my supervision styles because each of them provided me new experiences, pushed me when I needed it, and offered sincere support of my endeavors. These supervisors still serve as professional references for me in job searches, have nominated me for awards and positions of service for national organizations. Their professional values are similar—a combination of the importance of fun, adaptability to change, confidence and competence, and the ability to respond to the changing landscape of the field better than other generations. My angle was that I worried the most about what these supervisors thought of me. I wanted to be like them; therefore, I felt compelled to consistently exceed their expectations. I had regularly scheduled one-on-one meeting times with these supervisors when I could update them on my work and ask for feedback. It was with these supervisors that I felt the most confidence in my work because I truly knew what their expectations were and how to meet those expectations.

I have also had a couple supervisors who fit into the Baby Boomer generation. These supervisors were considerably more "hands-off" in their approach; while I did not ever feel micro-managed by them, I felt the need for more feedback. Each of these supervisors seemed approachable when needed, but I did not have the ongoing, regular one-on-one meetings that I have learned I need, in order to gain the confidence that I was truly accomplishing the goals set out for me and my position. While I was given more freedom to accomplish tasks the way I felt was best, I did not have the relationship with these supervisors that I felt like I could ask for ongoing feedback. It was with these supervisors that I worried more when it came to evaluations. In hindsight, this was because I did not have that ongoing exchange of information and ideas that I had with those of Generation X.

Because of these experiences, my foundation for supervision expectations has been laid. I know now that for me to feel best supervised, I need a relationship in which I feel that I can ask for and receive ongoing feedback. While I do not wish to be micro-managed, I want to be able to give consistent updates on my work. This way, I can get the ongoing feedback that I wish to receive. To me, this also means that I have the opportunity to meet consistently in one-on-one closed meetings. Ironically, in these relationships, I have fewer topical things to discuss in meetings because we have opportunities to share ideas, discuss problems, and find solutions prior to and between the one-on-one meeting times.

To summarize, the supervision that has worked best for me has been ongoing, not confined only to evaluation time for feedback. I truly value the supervision relationships that have felt professionally comfortable.

Laura E. Ulmer, M.Ed.
Director of Student Conduct & Academic Integrity
Old Dominion University

Table 2.2 reviews the key differences in generational influences and work styles, attitudes and priorities.

Table 2.2 Generational Influences in Work Styles, Attitudes, and Priorities

Generation	Shaped by...	Work styles, attitudes, and priorities
Matures	Children of war and depression, conformity as a ticket to success, risk averse, early marrying.	America's newest and most affluent-ever seniors, they remained in the workplace of choice and necessity.
Boomer	Came of age rebelling against the worldly blueprints of their parents, civil rights, flower power, and Woodstock.	Retirement eviscerated by the Great Recession, postpone retirement, preparing for elder years of wisdom and meaning.
Gen Xer	Latchkey childhood, soaring divorce rates, AIDs, economic hardship.	Free agency over corporate loyalty, would rather volunteer than vote, dependent care benefits critical as parenting was delayed for this group.
Millennial	Social media, access to information, 1st generation digital natives, record high youth unemployment rates.	Flexible workplace, work–life balance, mentorship and career advancement programs.

Adapted from *Generations in History* (2015)

Conclusion

As leaders and managers, we do well to listen with a thoughtful ear to what can be insightful, fresh ideas and viewpoints across the generations that make up the current workforce, rather than limiting or diminishing contributions based upon clichéd, damaging stereotypes. By taking the time to better understand the unique needs and experiences of our staff from across the generations, we position ourselves to capitalize on the talents of our workforce.

As our final *Example from the Expert* from Dr. Richard Pattenaude, President and CEO of Ashford University so astutely points out, "A good leader should be careful to not over-generalize about the enduring and fixed nature of generational characteristics and patterns...even as we acknowledge [their] solid truth...generational differences are not deterministic."

EXAMPLE FROM THE EXPERT—
2.3: ALL GENERATIONS EXIST WITHIN EACH GENERATION

We hear a lot about the emerging need to manage the mix of multi-generations in our lives, businesses, and organizations. Whether it is Millennials, Matures, Gen Xer's or Boomers, each has distinct characteristics. A question that I wrestle with is *to what extent do I acknowledge and integrate that analysis as I lead a large, complex university?* My own experience suggests two refinements to the strict generational analysis will be helpful without undermining the value of the basic concept of generational differences.

First, to me it seems that all generations exist within each generation. So, while social and economic factors may greatly influence Boomers to be more driven, loyal, and focused, I know plenty of Boomers who are more like Matures. They tend to be quiet; humble in victory, stoic in defeat, as my dissertation advisor suggested. A few years back I offered an Associate Dean, a Boomer born in the early 1950s, the opportunity to have a broader but busier portfolio which had a clear and positive career path. He turned me down. Why, I asked? It's a great opportunity, although it would be disruptive to your life for a while for sure. (Remember when corporations moved people every two or three years as a management development initiative and simply assumed people would jump at the opportunity?). He said to me, "No Richard, I want to go back to my old job as a faculty member where life was more stable and predictable. I don't want an upwardly mobile career." Yow! I didn't know what to say, but at the same time, quietly admired his comfort and courage at being himself. He certainly wasn't acting like a Boomer. Many don't.

Second, a good leader should be careful to not over-generalize about the enduring and fixed nature of generational characteristics and patterns. I think most of us change over time. Each generation evolves as it ages. Age has a powerful impact on behavioral patterns. As Benjamin Disraeli once wryly noted, "A man who is not a liberal at 16 has no heart. A man who is not a conservative at 60 has no head." True or not politically, people do change their behavior as they age, learn life's lessons, get bruised a bit, and become typically more cautious.

I remember being a young Provost, outspoken, argumentative, an answer for everything, and always open to new ideas, and driven to get things done—now! Eventually a grizzled veteran administrator took me aside and growled, "You know Rich, in Connecticut we tend to go *around* the stone walls." It took me a day or two to fully absorb that, even longer to quit running *into* stone walls. But eventually I got it. To this day, I remain very careful around stone walls.

Generations are different, but as managers and leaders, we must be careful of the negative impact of simplistic overgeneralizing lest we end being the pointy-haired boss in the Dilbert cartoon who manages by clichés and generalities. Worse even is the risk of "typecasting" our staff. "Oh she's a Millennial, she won't be here in five years, so why promote her?" This limits opportunities and robs the organization of the value of an employee's full potential. *Generational differences are not deterministic even as we acknowledge they do have some solid truth to them.*

My own experience also suggests that no matter what their generation, individuals want to be heard and respected, want to be part of something larger than themselves, and want their work to have meaning. I suggest leaders should keep those ideas in mind, even as he or she struggles to get a young Millennial to delay their ski trip to complete a critical report for the Trustees.

Richard Pattenaude, Ph.D.
President and CEO,
Ashford University

DISCUSSION QUESTIONS

1. How do you see the generational differences playing into management conflicts within the workplace? Compare these differences to other factors such as socioeconomics, gender, race, ethnicity, culture, ability and geography. Do these differences always cause challenges or problems? What are some examples from your professional experience where any of these differences lead to deeper understanding and growth?

2. The authors push back some of the concept of seeing Millennials as problems in the higher education workforce. What has been your experience with how Millennials are considered in the workforce? Is there a bias? Is the bias warranted? Share your thoughts on this.

3. What are some employee qualities that transcend the issues of generation? Are there ideal employee qualities that a manager would seek out, separate from a person's generational affiliation?

4. Consider the concept of simultaneously "surrendering the cliché" and embracing the generational characteristics and patterns that are described in this chapter. What are some ways that you as a leader or manager can challenge yourself to elevate how you approach and work with staff across generations?

5. Notice the list of uncomplicated ways in which you can have success by embracing Millennial talent provided in the *Example from the Expert* in 2.1. Do these resonate with you? How will you begin implementing them with your staff?

Just One Thing

Erika Saracino
Clery Compliance Officer
University of California, San Diego

My dad was a high school basketball coach and PE teacher. He taught me that the greatest compliment someone can offer you is respect, and his teaching and leadership style really demonstrated this concept. It perhaps manifested itself most clearly to me when my dad retired several years ago and we threw him a surprise party. We invited former students and colleagues. They came from all over the country. I was amazed at the stories and gratitude that I heard about my dad. He was the consummate teacher and leader, in that he individualized what his students and players needed from him and offered them respect. He was tough when he needed to be tough. He offered a shoulder to cry on when tears needed to fall.

A leader needs to bring out the potential in every person that he or she leads and to recognize them as individuals with unique strengths. There's no one size fits all. A leader also needs to have humility, and to know when the individuals he or she leads can actually be the leader, and to step aside and clear the path so they can lead. A leader never tries to squash or belittle, and affords new opportunities for growth and development every moment of every day. **A great leader affords respect to the people he or she leads and, in turn, receives that respect right back.**

Chapter Three

Leadership versus Management

KEY TAKE-A-WAYS

- A key element of a strong leader is the ability to stay focused on the larger goals; even the larger purpose can be lost to those involved in the daily work. This requires a level of determination and delayed gratification to put off what is the easier path in trade for the larger reward down the line.
- Management requires an attention to detail, and the ability to plan and juggle multiple competing priorities with an apparent ease and calm. Successful managers possess a sense of equanimity and poise while sorting out what choice to make when competing needs collide in a department or division.
- Whether you have a stronger comfort level as a leader or manager, cultivating a balance of both the detailed and the wider perspectives gives the supervisor the ability to address the daily needs of the department while keeping focused on the overall mission and strategic vision. This skill is critical given that many higher education leaders often must act in both capacities.

INTRODUCTION

In listening to those who direct and oversee departments in colleges and universities, one of the frequent themes is the difference between leadership and management. Leadership typically focuses on larger directional issues, and movement of the department toward longer-term goals. Keywords here are new ideas and inspiring the masses. Management focuses more on the day-to-day needs of the department. Supervision works best when it balances these two competing needs; inspiring employees towards more distant goals and direction of the department versus ensuring everyday tasks are completed.

It has been famously stated that *Managers do things right, Leaders do the right thing.* In fact, leadership requires a flexibility of thought that the best managers may find challenging. We can certainly agree that the higher up the organizational chain one is positioned, the more (by volume and complexity) there is to consider. The leadership of a diverse workforce is just one facet of those considerations. Meanwhile, supervisors and managers address the day-to-day operational challenges faced within their multi-generational offices.

So, is this text written for an audience of leaders or managers? The answer is absolutely, both. Understanding the intersection of a new way to lead that is predicated on caring for a highly diverse and multi-generational workforce is fodder for both the most senior higher education leader and the most junior supervisor or manager.

Consider the college or university workplace a cross-country road trip. When taking a road trip, leadership focuses more on the goals, mission and desired outcome. What is the purpose of the trip? When do we need to arrive in order to stay on schedule? What are our overall cost limits for the trip? How would a successful trip be described? Who is ultimately responsible for the trip?

Management issues for the same trip involve monitoring the logistics and resources needed to accomplish the leadership goals. How many people will be in the car? How often can we stop? Where should we get the gas? How many hours each day should we drive? Who sits where in order to lessen conflict? How do we decide what music we will listen to on the trip?

Ideally, whether planning a cross-country road trip or serving as a director of a counseling center, goals are more likely to be accomplished in an efficient and effective manner when management and leadership work in tandem to achieve the overall objectives. Too much leadership, and the day-to-day tasks are lost. Too much management and we lose touch with the overall goal and mission. Leadership sets out the goals; management works to achieve these goals through logistics support.

Table 3.1 Leadership versus Management for Counseling Department

Leadership	Management
Focus on easy access to care for students in need 24/7. We want students who come into the office for help to be served quickly and without hassle.	Creation and implementation of intake and triage system that addresses emergency care, waitlists and assignment to a diverse set of therapists and counselors. Maintenance of afterhours on-call system.
Safe, confidential and trustworthy services.	Hiring wide range of clinicians including mental health counselors, psychologists and social workers from a diverse background. On-going staff meetings and supervision to ensure adherence to ethical standards.
Clear documentation that can be accessed during a crisis, addresses legal risk and provides an end of the year report on services delivered.	Investment in electronic record management systems.
All students aware of range of services offered by counseling center.	Variety of outreach programs on topics of suicide prevention, eating disorders, overview of services, depression/anxiety, substance abuse. Programming offered online, in brochures, at orientation, in classrooms and residence halls.

EXAMPLE FROM THE EXPERT— 3.1: LEADERSHIP VERSUS MANAGEMENT

I am definitely a better leader than a manager. I have found that often the better you lead, the more likely you are to be "kicked upstairs" to management. We see this happen in all types of educational settings. How many times have we seen the best instructor taken from the classroom or the best counselor taken out of the provider role and made department heads to handle administrative duties? We enter these educational professions, whether instructional or student affairs, to work with students and often end up sitting at a desk detailing budgets, approving payrolls and writing policy, but having minimal contact with those that drew us to our careers.

There was a time when my official title was "Judicial Officer." My supervisor was very insistent that I be called a director and shared his experience at a previous institution where the judicial officer felt slighted and thought she was not on the same level as other department heads based on her lack of title as "Director of." The change was made for me and then I had the experience of learning major differences between management and leadership.

My daily work suddenly changed and the expectations of those above me changed. My performance measures changed from being good at providing a fair, firm and consistent student conduct process to focusing on developing the office—both staff and the services we offered; marketing these services including reframing the way in which the office's image was viewed by the campus; training others on my skill set—which I resisted, as I saw that as my personal work product, developed over many years with no assistance; preparing reports and designing assessments. What had been my primary role, working with students that had gotten off track and were making poor decisions, became secondary. I have had to learn to adjust my priorities to balance what is expected of me from above, with what I know needs to be done with those I supervise and the students I serve.

I prefer operating in the role of servant leader. I work *with* my staff, they don't work *for* me. I solicit their ideas. I listen to their concerns. We examine projects and services we provide as a group—including the student assistants—and openly discuss how each of our assignments and how we handle them impacts each other, so that we have synergy rather than conflict. Leaders inspire others to get things done. Leaders help others develop. A servant leader puts the team members first and never asks of others what they wouldn't do themselves. A servant leader fosters an environment where others feel free to question and to suggest or try new ways of approaching things. When things don't go as planned, we work through it. When the decisions of others outside our office negatively impact us, we heal ourselves. This healing most often includes a great deal of humor!

I'll take being a leader—preferably a servant leader—any day, to being just a manager. In our office, we have a shared vision of success. We know that we are there to help students. Sometimes that means tough love and a student missing out on a prime registration time or taking a time-out from enrollment. We deal with angry people on a daily basis. But that shared vision includes the foresight to know that we are doing what is best for that student in the long run.

To sum it all up, I think management is about the organization: following regulations, documenting how or when tasks are done, measuring the quality and quantity of services provided. Leadership is about people: those you serve, those you supervise, meeting each one where you find them and helping them grow.

Peggy S. Scott, Ed.D., LPC-S
Director, Student Rights and Responsibilities Office
Stephen F. Austin State University

THOUGHTS ON LEADERSHIP

For most, leadership is how a director or supervisor envisioned their job before they were hired. Few take on this type of position with hopes of spending their days talking to staff about arriving at work on time and keeping old food from accumulating around their desk areas. Leadership means being the captain of the boat, inspiring your sailors to work in cooperation towards the goals and mission of the department. Leaders are charismatic and inspirational. They focus a bit more on the where and the why, than on the how and the what.

Leadership can be lonely at times. A key element of a strong leader is the ability to stay focused on the larger goals. This requires a level of determination and delayed gratification to put off what is the easier path in trade for the larger reward down the line. Employees sometimes look for guidance and respond well to being inspired and driven toward a goal. Other times, it can feel like trying to herd a group of cats to a goal. A leader should have patience and a sense of steadfastness when it comes to keeping others on track toward a distant goal. There are times when employees won't feel like the immediate sacrifice, or that hard work is worth accomplishing the larger goal. It is here where a strong leader keeps their eyes firmly focused on the end result as well as inspiring others to keep working towards a goal they may have lost faith in achieving.

Sometimes in leadership, the accomplishment of a goal can feel like the mythological story of Sisyphus who was forever compelled to roll an immense boulder up a hill, only to watch it roll back down. A leader understands that unlike the story of Sisyphus, progress arrives in due time and inspires their team when they find it difficult to roll the boulder up one more time. In his book, *Management of the Absurd*, Richard Farson aptly describes this phenomenon when he says *"the real strength of a leader is the ability to elicit the strength of the group."* (1997, p. 144)

37

Table 3.2 Leadership Qualities and Examples from Popular Media

Leadership Quality	Examples from Popular Media
1. Ability to focus on bigger picture and keep individual staff informed and focused on the larger departmental goals without becoming bogged down with details or obstacles.	• Frodo Baggins from *Lord of the Rings* focused on overall mission • Albus Dumbledore from *Harry Potter* book series
2. Charismatic and inspirational. Whether it is a quiet confidence or outspoken rock star, leaders tend to have qualities that inspire others and point steadily in the direction the department needs to move towards.	• *Xena the Warrior Princess* from the 90s TV series • Captain Malcom Reynolds from *Firefly* TV show • Alec Baldwin's character from *Glengarry Glen Ross*
3. Understanding of larger strategic goals and the politics of the university. Leaders have an instinctual awareness of when to raise their heads against the wave and when to duck under and fight that wave another day.	• Tyrion Lannister from the HBO series *Game of Thrones* • Professor Charles Francis Xavier from the movie *X-Men*
4. Ability to tolerate isolation and stay focused on the mission during times where support is lacking.	• Yoda from *Star Wars* in the swamp on Dagobah • Buffy from the TV series *Buffy the Vampire Slayer*
5. Ability to rally others to action even when the day-to-day challenges seem like they are overwhelming and the end.	• Walter White from *Breaking Bad* TV series • Rick Grimes from the *Walking Dead* TV series

THOUGHTS ON MANAGEMENT

Few join a college or university to be in the role of policing staff behavior within a department and overseeing budgetary requests for office supplies. Management is the day-to-day focus on the operational minutiae that must work in tandem to achieve the strategic goals of the department. Management supports leadership in the same way that Scotty from *Star Trek* always seemed to be trying to make sure Captain Kirk had the power and weapons he needed to accomplish his goals. Leadership without management working in support of its goals is simply someone writing down their wants and dreams on paper. While the left side of Table 3.1 includes some inspiring and lofty goals for a counseling center, these goals would have little meaning without the practical scaffolding in place that makes up the right side of the chart.

Management is often the unsung hero when describing supervisor and director traits. Management requires an attention to detail, and the ability to plan and juggle multiple competing priorities with an apparent ease and calm. Successful managers possess a sense of equanimity and poise while sorting out what choice to make when competing needs collide in a department. Managers don't have the luxury of falling back to the larger mission and ignoring the realities of staffing, budget balancing, and demands from the students, faculty and staff that never quite seem to relent.

For a manager, being detail-oriented and able to multi-task while remaining calm, cool, and collected in the face of difficulty is a top priority. An ability to interpret the Captain Kirk-like ramblings of a leader and translate them into action is the mark of a great manager. A leader may come in to request an increase in availability for academic tutors to serve students during finals. The manager's task is then trying to work with the existing tutors and their own holiday plans that may not allow them to work overtime or accommodate additional requests from students. The manager doesn't become overwhelmed with the task, but instead attempts to solve the problem given the parameters they have to work with on the job.

Table 3.3 Management Qualities and Examples from Popular Media

Management Quality	Examples from Popular Media
1. Ability to multitask and obtain the resources from a variety of departments and locations to ensure uninterrupted services delivery.	• Zoe Washburn from the TV series *Firefly* • Leslie Knope from the TV series *Parks and Recreation*
2. Ability to make sacrifices in order to prioritize the task at hand.	• Morpheus from the movie *The Matrix* • Giles from *Buffy the Vampire Slayer*
3. Remaining calm, cool and collected in order to portray equanimity and keep the department level-headed and on an even keel.	• Carol from the TV series *The Walking Dead* • Dolores Umbridge from the *Harry Potter* book series
4. Working with others to build a coalition toward keeping everyday work tasks smooth and on-mission. Encourage sharing of ideas to increase teamwork.	• Fred from the TV series *Scooby Doo* • Brad Pitt's character from the movie *Inglourious Basterds*
5. Ability to analyze existing data and make adjustments to improve efficacy and effectiveness of operations.	• The Bobs from the movie *Office Space* • Vizzini from the movie *The Princess Bride*

39

LEADERSHIP AND MANAGEMENT IN TANDEM

For a leader, being detailed, orientated or focused on the exact resources that can be brought to task on the current project typically are secondary items and more the remit for those with a management focus. Leadership and management must work hand in hand to both inspire the office to move towards the larger, big-picture goals while keeping the day-to-day logistics of the office functioning. The leader knows the department needs a t-shirt cannon to wow the students at the orientation and help gain better visibility for the department. The manager knows on what budget line to set aside the payment for the t-shirt cannon so that the auditors won't ask why the counseling department needed to purchase a t-shirt cannon. (True story!)

EXAMPLE FROM THE EXPERT— 3.2: REFLECTIONS FROM A FORMER MARINE AND UNIVERSITY PRESIDENT

As I reflect on my role as past President and CEO of a graduate school of the social and behavioral sciences and on the journey: Twenty years of experience as a higher educator, two masters degrees and a doctoral degree in order for this to come to fruition, there were many inspirational moments along the way which made my path possible; I would like to share here a few stories which made a difference in my full understanding of what it has meant to be a manager and leader of people. *And, yes, I do believe that there is a distinct difference.*

Some of my early lessons on management and leadership occurred during the time I served as a United States Marine. My Military Occupational Specialty, also known as "MOS," was as a 2542 or a Communications Center Operator. I had the honor to safeguard some of the most sensitive top-secret documents in the world. My job as manager was to lead four junior Non-Commissioned Officers on a Communications Center shift. I reported to a Second Lieutenant relatively new in his role, who depended on me to provide him with guidance based on our operations.

I remember one incident when a junior employee of mine was asked to provide a highly sensitive document to a senior ranking officer. We determined that the officer did not have clearance to pick up this particular document. The junior Marine simply did not know what to do. I approached the window where the officer stood and then told him that we were not authorized to provide this document to him. Although he insisted on receiving the document, I declined his request, explaining that he was not authorized. The officer informed me that he would be reporting me because I did not follow orders. I spoke with my Lieutenant who was on duty, to let him know what occurred. I was then commended for following policy and procedure and for appropriately managing the situation.

Lesson learned... in every aspect of work life there are rules, regulations, and policies. I explained to my junior Marine that when in doubt... go back to the policy... go back to the procedure, and follow it. This is the best way to manage. By the way, that Second Lieutenant I spoke of... he is a retired Colonel living in Colorado Springs, CO and is a dear friend to this day. He always tells me that I was an important part of his formation as a leader in his early days in the Marine Corps. Never underestimate how individuals can make an impact in your life. I certainly do not.

Relating to leadership... One of my early positions in higher education was as an academic counselor for a large university. Working in a student services department can be rather challenging because of the level of responsibility to ensure that students are supported throughout their degree program. This involves possessing an understanding of every program offered by the institution, transcript evaluation, collaborating with other institutions concerning the transferability of credits, counseling the student on scheduling, dropping and re-entering students, and being able to fill gaps in their schedule. There are many variables to consider when one serves in this role, the most important one being to ensure that a student is on track for graduation.

What I learned during this period of time as an academic counselor is a belief that a good counselor should treat every student as if they are their only student.

I truly believe that the most influential position I have held in higher education—and in an ancillary way helped to prepare me to be a president of a university—was my role as an academic counselor. I learned infinite elements about the student's journey which prepared me to be an astute, knowledgeable, and sensitive president. When I speak to my leadership team about my experiences, it seems to touch them. They want to know that their president is a real human being, that I have had experiences similar to theirs. It is easier for them to follow in the footsteps of someone who is like them.

So in the end, every encounter and situation means something. They are all learning experiences which can propel us higher to our true being as a leader or send us in a trajectory of not being as successful as we would hope. It is our individual choice to thoughtfully use these experiences throughout our career; but is that not a wonderful thing? No one can take away our ability to make choices or decisions as we navigate through life.

Charlita Shelton, Ph.D.
Past President & CEO,
University of the Rockies

MANAGER OR LEADER?

Carol and Iris

Iris is a Gen X manager of a small Student Affairs office. She and Carol have previously worked as peers, and the two have a solid working relationship that is built upon mutual respect. Carol is a Boomer who is dealing with both her parents' declining health. Most recently, Carol has moved her mother, who has dementia, into a skilled nursing facility. Iris sees Carol struggling with one painful decision after another where her parents are concerned. Iris has offered a great deal of flexibility regarding Carol's attendance and timeliness. They check in with one another regularly and Iris is genuinely concerned for Carol and her parents.

Lately, Iris has observed that Carol had made some careless mistakes in her work, and demonstrates a generally poor attitude toward work. She is easily agitated and highly emotional. Iris struggles with how to approach Carol. One day, in an important meeting with external constituents, Carol makes inaccurate and inflammatory statements that reflect poorly on the department. Iris is incensed. As the department manager, she takes personal responsibility for the behavior of her staff and the reputation of her department.

Key Question: As her manager, what are Iris's priorities as she approaches Carol?

An important step that Iris takes in this scenario is to take some time. While she is highly frustrated, she understands that no good can come from reacting emotionally to Carol's misstep. She reminds herself that this is not about her, that this is about Carol.

After a weekend of reflecting upon what has occurred, Iris asks to meet with Carol. She explains clearly and calmly what has occurred, and why it is problematic. But, most importantly, Iris focuses on the very competent professional she knows Carol to be. Iris remembers that this behavior is a deviation from Carol's usual way of behaving. By focusing on the impact of Carol's struggles with her parents, Iris externalizes the problem so that she can help support Carol in addressing it. She expresses sincere empathy for Carol's situation and clearly explains that the behavior is not acceptable. Iris tells Carol that she is worried for her wellbeing. She has come to the meeting prepared with information on their Employee Assistance Program. Iris asks Carol if she would be willing to call the EAP for an appointment. She offers to call together with Carol, if that would be helpful. She also asks Carol if it would be okay with her for them to check in over the next few weeks to see if and how seeing the EAP Counselor is helping to support Carol.

Carol begins seeing a counselor to help her deal with the stresses of her responsibility to her parents and, over time, is able to communicate about the impact of her parents on her as a whole person. The relationship between Iris and Carol is strengthened and Carol has a clear sense that she is a valued employee. She trusts that she will be treated fairly, even through adversity, and becomes a more engaged employee as a result of this experience.

In the case of Iris and Carol, is Iris manager or leader? The answer is both: She understands her responsibility to address Carol's concerning behaviors, but she also holds a vision for the future that Carol (and other employees) can share. In this vision, employees are valued as both technical contributors to departmental functions and as individuals.

Table 3.4 Generational Characteristics: Leaders and Managers

Generation	Leadership	Management
Millennial	May have good ideas and passion, but lack experience and gravitas to inspire others to follow their steps.	Not always known for their detail-oriented approach to daily work. They would manage better when they have a buy-in to the end goal.
Gen Xer	Often have big dreams and big hearts mixed with a practicality. Often work well, inspiring others to tasks.	Buy-in to the overall project is likely needed here. Gen Xer's typically have an aversion to the status quo and simply doing things because they are told.
Boomer	Often well liked and inspirational in their leadership abilities.	Have longer history of experience working for the company and monitoring worker performance.
Mature	May be seen as too out of touch and could be difficult to inspire others given their energy, age and potential 'been there, done that' attitude.	Often excel here. They are familiar with big business requirements for the minutiae of day-to-day operations. Often a lingering desire to please and accommodate.

EXAMPLE FROM THE EXPERT—
3.3: LEADERSHIP AND MANAGEMENT MARCH HAND IN HAND

For many, the distinction between leadership and management may be a bit murky. I have been fortunate to work for a number of outstanding supervisors over the years, and most of them were both strong leaders and managers. When someone is doing both roles well, it can be hard to tell where one role ends and the other begins.

I started to think more about these two terms during a period of time when I reported to an interim Dean of Students. This supervisor was an experienced higher education professional, but did not have any traditional student affairs experience. As you can imagine, a number of us wondered what it would be like. While we knew and had enjoyed working with this colleague, having an "outsider" (at least by our traditional definitions) caused us some degree of uncertainty.

In the end, the experience was a very positive one in many ways. The question was—what made it work? What were the takeaways from this experience? Here are a few:

1. Leadership abilities are highly transferrable
   Student affairs divisions are full of specific, specialized knowledge. Medical requirements, housing assignments, student codes, Title IX, parking regulations, performer contracts... the list goes on. It was not important for our Interim Dean to know all this from the start. What they needed to know was, what does this group of professionals need to make them the most effective? What motivations, what resources, and what support? The Director-level staff in the division knew their jobs and their functional areas very well, but they still needed someone to lead them. Not someone to pick through room selection booklets and calendars of events, but someone to say "Let's get this stuff done now, and let's be the best division we can be." Not high-content language, but motivating language. Good leaders can do that—pull us out of the minutiae and get us looking at our direction, speed, and momentum.

2. Leaders from the outside can be perspective-changing
   Lots of people feel a level of fear when someone "from the outside" comes in. However, these moments can be opportunities. When someone with real leadership skills helps us look at how we do things, and when we let our defenses down, there can be powerful change. Even if part of our practice is time-tested, having someone with a new perspective can be refreshing. The act of explaining to the Interim Dean how the conduct process worked (how timelines are created, how decisions are reached, and so on) helped me to get back to the basics and explain the "whys" more than ever. I likely was defensive from time to time, but it became clear that they were not looking to manage things, but rather wanted me to be a better, more informed leader.

3. Leadership is harder to identify (and teach) than managing
   To me, management has a great deal to do with functional area-specific knowledge. When I managed a pizza house, I knew a great deal about making the food, stocking the prep areas, and managing priorities. Definable skills, and ones I could impart to others and manage quite easily. Leadership can be a bit harder to define. We all know some people who

45

just "have it." That ability to positively motivate people at their core. That ability to wake up a room or an office by their presence. That ability to pick up folks who are worn out and tired and help them over the next hurdle. Can these things be taught? Surely. However, the "spark" of a great leader is sometimes just not there. Assessing if someone has that spark is so helpful in finding the best role for them in your division or department.

In the end, it has been highly instructive for us to reflect on our experience with our Interim Dean. Leadership and management do often march hand in hand, but they are certainly not the same thing.

Jason Buck
Associate Dean of Students,
New England College

BRINGING IT ALL TOGETHER

As in the case of Iris and Carol, there are times when a college or university may not have the luxury of having both a dedicated leader and manager in a particular department or on a given project. This presents the challenging opportunity for the leader/manager to play both roles, doing their best to navigate and attend to the requirements of both. The vast majority of readers can think of a time when they experienced a similar situation. Indeed, managers and supervisors may find that the best proving ground for moving into leadership roles happens when they are stretched to play both roles. To this end, supervisors are more effective when they approach their work with an awareness of how these two issues connect, and when it is more appropriate to be leadership- or management-focused when working with an individual employee.

There are times when employees are in need of a reminder about the overall mission of the department and the importance of viewing their work performance against these higher-order, noble goals. A supervisor with strong leadership abilities may emulate the image of a football coach inspiring a team to dig in hard to overcome the opposition during a second half. The supervisor focuses on being inspirational and supportive to assist the employee to stay focused on the importance of their work as it relates to the overall mission. An example of this might be a supervisor talking to an employee in an academic tutoring department. The emphasis for the meeting is on the overall retention goals of the university and ensuring the employee's actions are seen in this context.

In other scenarios, it would be reasonable to work with the employee with a focus on day-to-day management needs. In our example, an academic tutor may become overwhelmed with the number of students that are requesting appointments. A good manager helps the tutor better delegate their time in order to triage appointments. While this scheduling discussion is done best by a supervisor competent in management, the behavior being shaped (balancing multiple appointments) directly impacts the students' access to assistance, and in turn, to their academic success and departmental retention goals.

Whether you have a stronger comfort level as a leader or manager, cultivating a balance of both perspectives gives you the ability to address the daily needs of the department while keeping focused on the overall mission and strategic vision. As the old question reminds us: Which came first, the chicken or the egg? In the end, it doesn't really matter. What matters is that both the chicken and egg exist in the cycle. A supervisor or director would do well to be aware of management needs with their employees. A supervisor or director who has excellent management skills should consider finding ways to implement leadership approaches within their department and with their employees.

EXAMPLE FROM THE EXPERT— 3.4: WIN THE BATTLE AND THE WAR

I started a position as a director of counseling and found myself quickly aware of changes that needed to be made within the counseling center. The clinical staff were writing notes by pen and paper and had an aversion to using the computer systems. Charts were not searchable and often contained spelling errors and were hard to read. Appointments were also written down by hand and kept in a scheduling book on the front desk.

This was a new job for me and I immediately wanted to make a positive impression and demonstrate some leadership and vision by pushing the department forward towards the Titanium electronic data system. This provided an easy-to-use ability for the office to "go green" and vastly improve the accessibility and readability of the treatment notes and records we kept at the counseling center. It also offered the ability to replace the inefficient handwritten scheduling book that lived on the office manager's desk. Staff often copied down their schedules and borrowed the book, making it hard to take new appointments or have other staff review their schedule. The new Titanium system would solve all of these problems.

Some of the staff raised concerns about the security and privacy of these computerized records, as they didn't have much experience with electronic record databases. I nodded at these concerns and proceeded to push forward with the Titanium plan. I assumed any change would bring about some dissension in the ranks and reassured myself this is why they hired me; to make substantial changes and bring the department up to current industry standards.

The change went well, and after five years there were no complaints or questions about the system. Staff enjoyed the ease of the new charting systems and how quickly they could schedule and adjust their appointments. Security concerns proved unfounded and there were added unseen benefits in terms of having a more robust system to review intern and practicum students' notes. The adaptation of our pen and paper notes to Titanium was an undisputed good move for the department.

Looking back on these, ten years later, I feel like I displayed the qualities of leadership but lacked the management skills to better address and hear the concerns the staff had around change. While the change was positive in the end, the way I pushed forward the update to the electronic database system cost me in terms of trust and collaboration. Already ten years younger than most staff in the department, I found myself in many additional conflicts, many of which could be seen as conflicts between Gen X and Boomer lines.

If I could go back in time, I would have waited a few more months and formed work groups to discuss the concerns around the change to a new chart and scheduling system. Building collaboration by listening to staff, rather than simply dismissing their concerns, would have been a more effective long-term approach. While the Titanium update was the right course of action, I should have been more attuned to how the staff reacted to change.

Brian Van Brunt, Ed.D.
The NCHERM Group

DISCUSSION QUESTIONS

1. What is your understanding of the difference between leadership and management? Give some examples of each.

2. What quality is more important for a director or department head to possess, leadership or management? Think of some examples where you have had a director, supervisor or department head that focused more on leadership. What were the benefits of this? What were the limitations? Consider the same questions with a supervisor, director or department head who was more manager than leader.

3. Share some stories where micro-management of job tasks made it more difficult to stay effective and efficient in your everyday work. What are some ways to address micro-management with a director, supervisor or department head?

4. Have you had an experience with a department that had two separate people, one a leader, the other a manager? How did that process work for the department?

5. Give some examples where generational issues between a manager or leader had a negative impact on the department where you worked? What are some positive examples where generational differences led to better outcomes for the department?

Just One Thing

Lisa Medina, M.B.A., CFE
Associate University Registrar & Director of Student Records
Ashford University

Leadership is not complicated. In fact, there are only a relative few uncomplicated principles by which successful leaders abide (take a peek in nearly any leadership book, and you will find them: respect, humility, love, and service). However, one should not confuse uncomplicated with easy. It requires strength and courage to stand on these basic leadership principles when it counts. So if I were to impart just one slice of wisdom to fellow leaders, it would be this: develop a deep understanding of your values, and spend your energy executing them consistently and effectively. Don't overcomplicate it!

Chapter Four

Three Theories
Taking a Page from Psychology to Manage Across Generations

KEY TAKE-A-WAYS

- The **Humanistic, Person-Centered Approach**, when a supervisor better understands how the employee feels about their work performance, and the potential conflicts and challenges in their day-to-day experiences, gaining valuable insight and putting "money in the bank" that can help build trust and improve the likelihood of future interventions being effective when addressing problem behaviors or seeking to bring about change.
- **Narrative and Story** have always been part of the human condition. Their utility in supervision is to help the manager to better support the employee in understanding their own story in the environmental context of their development. This provides the employee with the opportunity to engage more fully with others and have the needed self-esteem and hope to successfully engage in change.
- **Positive Psychology** suggests that we help employees build on a positive experience to develop healthy traits and to ultimately create or connect with healthy institutions and communities. The difference between people who are successful and those who are not often depends on how they see failure. Supervisors can help employees see failure or mistakes as temporary setbacks along the longer journey of workplace success.

While our goal is not to turn supervisors, managers and directors into therapists, there are some useful theories, techniques and concepts in the literature and practice of clinical psychology that offer perspectives in managing difficult situations in the workplace and addressing the challenges of managing across the generations.

Three approaches to helping will be discussed: the humanistic, person-centered approach to therapy first outlined by Carl Rogers (1961, 1980); the narrative approach to therapy created by White and Epston (1990); and the positive psychology and flow theory approaches first suggested by Seligman (2006) and Csíkszentmihályi et al. (1988). Each approach offers supervisors a unique approach to managing change and addressing conflict in the workplace.

1. THE HUMANISTIC, PERSON-CENTERED APPROACH

The principle of the Humanistic, Person-Centered approach is captured in the following quote from Carl Rogers (1961): "When someone understands how it feels and seems to be me, without wanting to analyze me or judge me, then I can blossom and grow in that climate" (p. 62). Two concepts central to understanding Roger's therapy technique are Congruence and Empathy. These are the essential qualities for a supervisor seeking to encourage change in their employees. Empathy means seeing the world from an employee's eyes, understanding from their perspective. Congruence is about the supervisor conveying a sense of genuineness and authenticity to the employee. We tend to trust those whom we can understand and who seem honest and direct about their goals.

For a manager or director, establishing empathy relates to the supervisor taking the time and effort to put their agenda and goals aside for a moment and, instead, truly reflect on the perspective and worldview of the employee. This is not intended to take away from the importance of having an agenda or goals for supervision. Rather, we are suggesting the supervisor begin the supervision process from this vantage point. As Stephen Covey writes in his book *The Seven Habits of Highly Effective People* (1990), first understand and then be understood. When the supervisor takes the time to understand the employee's perspective, they gain valuable insight into how the employee approaches their job.

When a supervisor better understands how the employee feels about their work performance, and the potential conflicts and challenges in their day-to-day experiences, they gain valuable insight and put "money in the bank" that can help build trust and improve the likelihood of future interventions being effective when addressing problem behaviors or attempting to bring about change. This starts with a willingness of the supervisor to focus on their employee's perspective. An associated benefit to this approach is the modeling of empathetic listening from supervisor to employee. When we do this for those in our care, we teach them how to do this for others. As Rogers (1961) puts it, "An empathetic way of being can be learned from empathetic persons" (p. 150). This is particularly important when reflecting on generational differences in our staff where the skill of empathy may be lacking or may not have been taught, and is directly translatable to their interactions with students.

If empathy is the car, active listening is the gasoline that allows the car to run. Active listening is the ability to understand the underlying message communicated from employee to supervisor. The supervisor conveys an ability to listen in a non-judgmental manner and allows the employee to share their perspective, free of defensiveness and hesitation.

Imagine a drinking glass. If the employee comes into supervision with a gallon's worth of liquid and sees that you have only a drinking glass, they will hold back because they know you won't be able to handle the volume of information they need to share. When a supervisor adopts an open, non-judgmental, active listening-based stance, it is as if they bring a gallon jug to the supervision. This conveys to the employee a willingness and capacity to receive as much information as they are willing to share.

As the supervisee becomes more comfortable with their supervisor's ability to listen, trust is established and it is more likely the employee will share additional information, and respond positively to suggestions for change in the future. Employees are more comfortable sharing their perspective when they are passionate and feel sure of themselves. When a supervisor provides a safe and nurturing environment for the employee to share their worldview, it allows for the employee to feel comfortable revealing their more protected, and less well-defined views on their work performance.

Carl Rogers summed up these ideals best in his book *A Way of Being* (1980):

> "[Empathetic listening] means the therapist senses accurately the feelings and personal meanings that the client is experiencing and communicates this understanding to the client. When functioning best, the therapist is so much inside the private world of the other that he or she can clarify not only the meaning of which the client is aware but even those just below the level of awareness. This kind of sensitive, active listening is exceedingly rare in our lives. We think we listen, but rarely do we listen with real understanding, true empathy. Yet listening, of this very special kind, is one of the most potent forces for change that I know." (p. 116)

Too often, supervision is seen as simply holding an employee to a set of standards and objectively reciting areas of compliance and non-compliance on work tasks. Yet, more often than not, successful supervision is about what Rogers mentions above. It is a caring, empathetic listening, an intimacy, a sharing. It is within this environment that lasting change occurs.

The added value of a positive supervisor–supervisee relationship is the potential for the supervisee to believe they will be able to form these kinds of positive relationships with others as well. The active listening and support offered by an experienced supervisor provides an example for employees in order to improve their own social skills and increase their chances of success when they attempt to form connections on their own. Again, Rogers (1961) writes, "If I can provide a certain type of relationship, the other person will discover within himself the capacity to use that relationship for growth, and change and personal development will occur" (p. 33).

When encouraging connection to others, the supervisor may also want to adopt the approach used by social workers and case managers in order to help direct the client toward more positive choices and overcome obstacles. This involves building from existing strengths in order to help develop better connections to others. Table 4.1 offers some opportunities for managers and leaders to begin exploring potentials for empathy across the generations. Remember, any time you make generalizations about an entire group of people, there is the potential to get it wrong when it comes to the particular individual in question. Connection and empathy requires active listening, patience and a willingness to adjust perceptions and assumptions.

Table 4.1 Opportunities to Empathize across Generations

Millennial	Gen Xer	Boomer	Mature
Frustration at being called a Millennial and being seen as lazy or disconnected	Balancing multiple responsibilities with family, children and caring for elderly parents	Concerns over retirement and what might be next for them in life	Fear of being seen as old and out of touch with others and technology
Annoyed at always being called to fix technology issues or be the "social media go-to person"	Potentially looking at second career or retooling to stay fresh and relevant	Frustration and conflict with Millennial generation and their perceived social media obsession	Frustrated at being seen as the grandparent of the office by younger staff
Unsure of job security given the market and worry how long they will be at their current job	Frustration at not being promoted or acknowledged for their skills and abilities	Exploring the idea of giving back and altruism as their children age and they see the end of their work life	Adjusting to age and stamina issues in terms of work performance

Millennial	Gen Xer	Boomer	Mature
Looking for a larger place in the world and meaning in their work	Wrestling with the concept of a mid-life crisis and looking for excitement and the next big thing	Frustration at being retired before they are really ready to be finished with their career; looking for meaning	Looking for larger meaning in work as they come back to work after retirement

EXAMPLE FROM THE EXPERT— 4.1: PERSON-CENTERED LEADERSHIP

Throughout my career I have practiced a person-centered approach to leadership. What this means to me is being emotionally present, being genuine and congruent—that my values are consistent with what I say and do. As a professor, I find this to be a most effective approach to facilitating learning with students, and as a community college board president, I notice this practice to be one that has resulted in my having a reputation for caring about people.

A person-centered approach makes it easier to meet people where they are at, whether you are working individually, or with groups.

As I reflect on more than 45 years in higher education, one of the things I notice about being at this stage in my career is that being older gives me credibility. I come in without doing anything in particular and I am granted power. You know that Spiderman saying, "With great power comes great responsibility"? I think at this stage, I am more aware that the time is now! I want to give it my best all the time. And as a bonus, students like my style of being more feisty and direct! I'm just less apologetic now and it's very freeing. With respect to generational differences, absolutely I see them. I think what is unfortunate, though, is that we hold people accountable for these differences despite the fact that they were not responsible for their making!

Here is an example: We are in an age where *consumerism is the constant message*. We are bombarded by it in the media, and this *comes in direct conflict with values of connection to others*. Is it the fault of the young person today that consumerism stands in direct conflict with connection to one another? Or, are they the product of this condition in our society?

This is a serious social issue—it cuts across many areas of diversity, not only generational. What is so powerful about a person-centered approach is that it provides a framework from which to approach people, individuals and groups. It says, "I come from a loving place. I care about you and your wellbeing."

Another example of a generational difference I see—in Millennials—is that they are *less interested in delayed gratification*. And this statement holds no judgment; maybe the lessened interest isn't a bad thing at all. I see young people making the choice to delay other kinds of things, like saving for a house, for example, in order to take what I would consider a trip of a lifetime. I see students who don't have jobs finding ways to travel and explore the world. Where the "value" question comes in is that, traditionally, we have regarded the ability to delay gratification as a virtue—it meant that you were mature and disciplined. So, from a generational perspective, we see young people demonstrating behaviors that stand in contrast to values that we have held—maybe still do. And this makes me think about a realization that I've made that the "time is now," and I think, *maybe these kids are on to something!*

Perhaps one of the most exciting things about generational differences is that they demonstrate the changes in our values as a society. Thinking about my early career as a teacher, at this time in my life I was often told that I was too sensitive and emotional. Some of the messages I received then indicated that there was one way, a single vision of what it means to be "professional," and that is to be "detached." To some degree, I think we still hold this today, and I know it needs to be changed. And so, it makes me happy to see young educators and leaders who are invested in taking a more person-centered approach and who understand that *to be detached is the very antithesis of what it means to be professional.*

A closing thought: A charge to younger generations of higher education leaders is to *use your power, whatever that power is, to raise questions that will lead to change.*

Maria Nieto-Senour, Ph.D.
President, San Diego Community College District Board of Trustees
Emeritus Professor and Former Program Director,
Community Based Block,
Department of Counseling and School Psychology,
San Diego State University

2. THE NARRATIVE APPROACH

The term "narrative therapy" was used by Australian family therapists Michael White and David Epston (1990) to define the way we all use stories to relate to our experiences. They suggested that people organize and give meaning to their experiences through the stories they tell. Individuals construct the meaning of life through stories and then treat these stories as the "truth" (Corey, 2001). Furthermore, "With every performance, persons are re-authoring their lives. The evolution of lives is akin to the process of re-authoring, the process of persons entering into stories, taking them over and making them their own" (Van Brunt, 2007, pp. 27–28). Through the process of helping patients examine their lives through the stories they tell, White and Epston found it possible to help those they worked with revise the telling of their stories in a manner that gave the patient more ownership and ability to gain dominion over negative past experiences. Narrative therapy helps individuals separate themselves from negative, unhelpful stories and gain an ownership of their life beyond subjugation. Narrative therapy encourages patients to adopt stories that free them from culture's oppression, and live out their alternative chosen stories (Besley, 2002). There is a strong power inherent in understanding, shaping, and then reconstructing others' thoughts and stories.

The process of externalizing the story is an essential aspect of the narrative approach to therapy. White (1988–9) wrote, "Externalizing is an approach to therapy that encourages persons to objectify, and at times, to personify, the problems that they experience as oppressive" (p. 5). White and Epston (1990) suggested that behavior, fears and worries must be first separated from the client prior to any attempt to reconstruct them. When a supervisee begins to experience a level of comfort sharing their stories, they can externalize them in order to allow the narrative to be more deeply explored and adapted by the supervisor. This approach is particularly effective when assisting staff who engage in problematic workplace behaviors, as it allows for free and open discussion of the behavior while separating it from the person. The result is an ability to address and resolve these behaviors without the perception of persecution on the part of the staff person.

Again, White and Epston (1990) write, "As persons become separated from their stories, they are able to experience a sense of personal agency; as they break from their performance of their stories, they experience a capacity to intervene in their own lives and relationships" (p. 16). This allows the supervisee to explore unique outcomes to their stories and obtain some freedom from the stories that previously restricted their options. This process of "storying" their experiences—adding description,

57

sensation, and detail to their creations—gives clues to the meaning they ascribe to their own life problems and experiences.

Poor Performance

Carol

Imagine an employee named Carol who works in academic advising. Carol is forty-two and struggles to balance her work life with her home life. She often comes to work late and has numerous student complaints related to missing or canceled appointments. Other staff in the department are annoyed at Carol since they often have to pick up tasks that she fails to complete. Carol often comes to supervision in tears and laments, "I just can't do this anymore. I feel like I'm giving 150% and no matter how hard I try, everyone feels as if I am letting them down. My husband is always yelling at me about money. I'm never home to take care of the kids. Everyone hates me at work. I just don't know what to do. I feel like I'm all tied up in ropes and I can't get free." For Carol, her story becomes so overwhelming for her that she becomes unable to act or take steps to bring about any change in her behavior.

One technique a supervisor can use is to encourage Carol to think about her problems while sitting in a chair across the room. Both Carol and the supervisor can look at her problems sitting in the chair and objectively have a conversation about the nature and specifics of what Carol's problems look like. This process is similar to what a mechanic does when repairing a carburetor. They do not try to fix it while it is still in the engine assembly. Instead, they remove the carburetor to better examine the nature of the problem.

When the problems are externalized, they can then be identified and given detailed characteristics. Carol and her supervisor can better understand the influence the problem has on her life. This is called mapping the problem. This mapping process examines how the problem influences the individual, their significant others, and their environment. When the stories themselves are identified and given detailed characteristics, the influence the problem has on the employee can then be mapped.

For Carol, trying to balance her work relationships, parenting responsibilities, family obligations, work performance, finances, and relationship with her husband would be the focus of her mapping. When she takes a step back from her stories about being overwhelmed, Carol can then tolerate greater exploration and alterations to these stories.

USING THE STORIES

Imagine that Carol has learned over time that she has to do everything perfectly. Stories that support these ideas are collected as she develops: I'm someone who cannot do everything right, I'm a failure as a wife, because I am not around enough I am also a failure as an employee, I'm not good enough. These stories become stifling and overwhelming. They remove options, restrict possibilities, and steer her life toward a self-fulfilling prophecy. The task of the supervisor here is to help Carol separate herself from these stories. The stories must be relieved of their power before the process of reconstruction can begin. The manager helps Carol set aside her negative stories through confrontation, hope, and by enlisting her in the creation of metaphors and imagery. Perhaps the supervisor and employee create an imaginary box where the negative stories can be temporarily laid down for the length of their sessions together. This jointly created metaphor should use descriptive terms and attempt to create a memorable, realistic image. The box could be strong and made of old wood, sturdy, and strapped with weathered iron bands. The supervisor could encourage the employee to create a key or talisman that would open the box, allowing its dark interior to accept the weight of the stories. The box could then be locked with a metallic turning click. With the stories safely locked away for a time, the employee is free to dream of other stories that put them in a more positive, advantageous light. This process of imagination, freedom, and creation creates the tapestry of narrative therapy. The individual's new view of self through the freshly authored stories helps them to overcome the status quo, to fully question what a person is, how problems can be defined, and under which conditions change occurs (Zimmerman & Beaudoin, 2002).

Kopp (1995) expanded some of the narrative therapy approach and suggested the importance of language and metaphor as therapeutic tools, suggesting that therapists attend specifically to the metaphors and analogies that clients use within sessions. These narrative pieces offer a crucial connection to the client's inner worldview. Raymond Corsini, encyclopedist and lexicographer in the field of psychology, wrote in the Foreword to Kopp's (1995) text:

> The client and therapist, acting like detectives, look for clues to understanding the essence of the mystery by exploring and transforming the client's metaphoric language, hoping to find something that has little significance either to the client or to anyone who does not know the secret of the metaphor, but which, when the secret is revealed, becomes the key that opens the lock of the door that has stood between the person and freedom. (pp. ix–x)

59

It is precisely these little clues that provide both the insight and framework toward solving the presenting problem existing between supervisor and employee. Kopp (1995) stresses the importance of engaging an individual's story through attending to the importance of language and metaphor as a tool for change.

He (Kopp, 1995) wrote of a patient who described her husband's lack of caring, coming and going from the house as he pleased and not looking for a job, with the metaphor "he barges into the house like a locomotive" (p. xiv). He then used this clue as an opportunity to create a dialogue about the situation. He questioned the client, "If he is a locomotive, what are you?" The patient clarified what the therapist asked and then replied, "A tunnel" (p. xiv). Kopp then asked, "What if you could change the image so that it would be better for you, how would you change it?" The patient thought and then suddenly exclaimed, "I'd be the derailer!" (p. xv). This self-as-derailer metaphor then became a shared construct between the therapist and patient. It served as a focal point for the patient to shift from a passive model—the tunnel—to an active model, the derailer, and allowed the patient to visualize the potential of new, unique outcomes.

A six-step approach is reviewed here and discussed:

1. Notice metaphors
2. Explore the metaphor using the individual's language
3. Broaden the exploration through questioning
4. Assess feelings and emotions associated with the image
5. Use the metaphor as an agent of change
6. Bring the metaphor back to the presenting life problems.

Carol's Story Explored

Let's take Carol's example of being tied up with ropes. The Kopp (1995) model would have the supervisor first notice the use of metaphor and the language attached to it. Secondly, the metaphor could be explored: How many ropes are there? Are some thicker than others? What type of rope is it? Are they all similarly tight or are some ropes looser than others? At the third stage the metaphor is accepted by both supervisor and employee and may be expanded upon: When did these ropes first appear in your life? What things in your life tighten the ropes around you? Are there times the ropes don't feel as overwhelming? Has a rope ever broken? The fourth step would involve the therapist questioning: What must it feel like to be tied up and held in one place? How would it feel to escape the ropes? The fifth step would have the supervisor exploring other ways the ropes could be loosened: Is there a way to stop the person or persons who tied the ropes at first? What if the trapped person didn't pull as much on the ropes and just kind of let them loosen on their own? Could the trapped person ask for help to untie some of the ropes? The final step would connect the symbolism of the rope to the employee and explore the possible new ways of looking at their life and interaction with others: When else have you felt tied up in your life? How can you stop the ropes from being tied? How can you release the ropes when they are already tied around you? Who can help with the untying of the ropes? Would someone like a counselor or accessing the Employee Assistance Program (EAP) be helpful? Given that it is hard to untie many ropes at once, what are some ways to avoid that first rope becoming tied?

If an employee like Carol has trouble coming up with metaphors, the supervisor may help by offering stories and ideas that may inspire the employee to think more about their life in terms of options. Close (1998), who advocated that the therapist use stories, symbolism, and metaphor as treatment examples, described himself as a pastoral counselor, advocating for a Christ-like method of using parables and examples through teaching. He described his work with a female patient "to transcend the effects of [a] rather harsh and deprived childhood" (p. 59). She was rapidly becoming a recognized musician with a promising career, which was abruptly halted when she was involved in a plane crash and lost the use of her left hand, keeping her from playing the cello. Close told his patient a long story involving a rare and beautiful tree that had to overcome many difficulties; it was planted under a rock and a strong storm uprooted the tree. Through these experiences, the tree learned to grow again and became a nesting place for songbirds.

The story weaves in the importance of uniqueness, overcoming environmental traumas, and of loving others and being loved. Close's (1998) method connected with the heart of the client, an area beyond simply connecting with the mind. He gave the example of the difference between looking at sheet music and actually hearing a beautiful aria. The use of metaphor in supervision is a similar concept. The stories connect with the employee's heart, becoming long-lasting touchstones for their journey through life.

Table 4.2 Using the Narrative and Metaphor Approach

Notice the metaphor	The supervisor catches Carol's use of metaphor around the rope and makes a decision to use it to help her bring about change.
Explore the metaphor	What kind of rope is it? How did the person get tied up to begin with? Did it all happen at once or over time? How many ropes are there? Are there more ropes that might be tied around the person? These questions use Carol's language and encourage her to talk more about the image she has and to expand on it.
Expand the metaphor	Where do the ropes come from? What would happen if the person asked for help to untie the ropes? Can the person being tied up move or must they sit there? These questions expand the metaphor beyond what Carol originally thought and encourage her to broaden the concept.
Assess feelings and emotions	How does the tied up person feel about their situation? Do the ropes have feelings as well? How did the person come to be here? Are they trapped or free to leave? How does the person feel when more ropes are added? The questions are designed to help Carol begin to explore the obvious connection between herself and the person trapped by the ropes. Because the supervisor is only talking about the metaphor, Carol is likely to respond freely.
Metaphor as agent of change	Are there things the person could do before the first rope is tied? Could they walk away from the ropes altogether? Could the ropes be shaped or used in a more useful way? The questions here help connect Carol to the idea of alternative options available to her. As mentioned above about problems with direct questions, this approach allows Carol to explore the options in a more distant, creative manner that is more detached from the emotions she would feel if asked, "Can you just manage your stress and obligations better so you don't get overwhelmed?" On that level, Carol would likely be overwhelmed by emotions and anger. When using the metaphor of the person trapped by the ropes, there is an emotional distance that allows Carol to explore her options as an agent of change.
Apply the metaphor	The supervisor might ask Carol: How do the ropes give you insight into your situation? What are some other options you have besides struggling in desperation against the ropes? Is it worth trying to find a way to get out ahead of the ropes being tied around you? The opportunities for the questions are endless as we explore ways Carol connects with the person tied up with the ropes.

Conclusion

Narrative and story have always been part of the human condition. The purpose of their use in supervision is to help the manager learn to better help the employee own their story and understand it in the environmental context of their development. With an employee who is overwhelmed with their problems and unable to focus on action steps to improve their work performance, the utility of narrative theory can be found in its ability to help the employee re-author their story and gain a more positive sense of self. This provides the employee with the opportunity to engage more fully with others and have the needed self-esteem and hope that their life may be amenable to change.

Many times, the stories told by employees offer a useful key to understanding how they see the world. If an employee's world is an overwhelming and scary place, the narrative approach provides a key to unlock another way of thinking about their potential in the workplace. Dealing with generational diversity, one way to visualize this is for the supervisor to elicit stories and metaphors to better understand how the employee views their world in respect to their age cohort. As with appreciating any good story, the first step is listening with a curiosity and respect for the storyteller's perspective.

3. THE POSITIVE PSYCHOLOGY APPROACH

Martin Seligman founded the positive psychology approach in 1998. In modern psychology, treatment is normally focused on a client's symptoms and difficulties. In contrast, Seligman's post-modern work studies people who live happy and successful lives and looks to teach their strengths to others. The approach is highlighted by a quotation from the British philosopher Thomas Troward (1847–1916): "The law of floatation was not discovered by contemplating the sinking of things, but by contemplating the floating of things which floated naturally and the intelligent asking of why they did so."

Supervision has the potential to focus on where the employee is failing to reach performance goals or becomes engaged in conflict with those in the workplace. In fact, traditional approaches to management and leadership that are overly focused on failure will do well to take a cue from this approach. The positive psychology approach suggests that while we respond appropriately to the negative, we should spend an equal amount of time looking at the qualities that enable individuals and communities to thrive. It encourages us to seek ways to support and connect to positive influences and supportive communities.

For supervisors, the idea of simply giving their employees raises and more money shouldn't be seen as a universal solution to staff malaise or under-performance. We've all heard the saying that money doesn't equal happiness; however, this concept has been researched beyond a simple turn of phrase.

Wealth is only weakly related to happiness both within and across nations, particularly when income is above the poverty level (Diener & Diener, 1996). While money is certainly a motivator, it has been our experience that offering support, reassurance, praise and positive feedback tend to have a greater positive impact on an employee's attitude and performance.

Likewise, simply having more material things like an office with a window, the newest computer gadget or smartphone, or an increased travel and conference budget doesn't equate with job satisfaction. Activities that make people happy in small doses—such as shopping, good food and making money—do not lead to fulfillment in the long term, indicating that these have quickly diminishing returns (Myers, 2000; Ryan & Deci, 2000).

Supervisors make a mistake when they become singularly focused on identifying negative behaviors, monitoring employees for slip-ups, and trying to control their office like a police officer walking his beat. Although we need to fill out incident reports and hold employees accountable for their behavior, we must primarily attend to qualities that make our employees healthier and focus the positive attributes of those who overcome obstacles and manage their stress effectively. It is here that we will find ways to help other struggling employees overcome their difficulties. Positive psychology doesn't suggest replacing supervisory goals and objectives related to workplace performance, but instead to supplement them, and encourage supervisors to attend to employees' potential and see negative behaviors as speed bumps on otherwise positive journeys.

Happiness and Success

Happiness and success are such basic concepts that we often assume that they imply a common understanding. But what does it really mean to be happy and successful?

We find ourselves in supervision with employees who beat themselves up over a single bad performance indicator or interaction with a student. We find ourselves talking to employees who have many friends in the office and are well respected by colleagues, but can't seem to get ahead on their work assignments. What does it mean to be happy? What does it mean to be a success?

Research tells us that people who express gratitude on a regular basis have better physical health, optimism, progress toward goals, wellbeing, and help others more (Emmons & Crumpler, 2000). Likewise, people who witness others perform good deeds experience an emotion called "elevation," and this motivates them to perform their own good deeds (Haidt, 2000). Supervisors can use this information to create an office environment that emphasizes these types of activities.

A supervisor could try the following exercises with an employee. They could ask the employee to imagine that everything has gone well at work and encourage them to think about what it would feel like to accomplish their life dreams and goals. They could ask the employee to write down three good things that happen each day and think about the causes for these good things. These positive-focused activities and exercises could help shift the employee to a more optimistic way of seeing their work on a day-to-day basis.

Positive psychology suggests that we help employees build on a positive experience to develop healthy traits and to ultimately create or connect with healthy institutions and communities. An example might be an employee who likes interacting with the students in the front office. A supervisor helps the employee further develop traits that help them be even more effective in communicating with students and then increases the employee's job duties to involve more student interaction. The final piece may be helping the employee find other opportunities around campus to work with students, perhaps advising a club or intramural sports team.

The difference between people who are successful and those who are not, often depends on how they see failure. We can help employees see failure or mistakes as temporary setbacks along the longer journey of workplace success. How often do we remind staff that they are not alone in making these mistakes? Do we remind them that other employees have struggled to master job performance issues and have gone on to excel and flourish? That other staff have also had trouble making friends or have felt so angry with someone they wanted to hit that person, but have gone on to deal with those feelings and do well in a department?

When we talk with employees about failures being temporary setbacks, we often don't make it the conversation's primary focus. Although many of us would agree that we should encourage hope in those we supervise, how often do we actually focus our energy on it? In his book, *Making Hope Happen,* psychologist Shane Lopez (2014) describes the "Hope Cycle" as one that includes goals—an idea of where we want to go, agency—our ability to shape our lives, and pathways—finding appropriate routes from where we are to where we want to be. When we apply this concept to the workplace, we can agree that supervisors and staff, as well as departments and institutions, benefit when staff see hope in their future, and experience their work through the lens of the Hope Cycle.

Seligman (2006) suggests there are three kinds of happiness all people are able to achieve. The first is found through pleasant engagement, where the individual is encouraged to find as much positive emotion as they can around them. They are then encouraged to try to amplify and be mindful of these good things, savoring them and stretching them to last longer. Some of us are better than others appreciating the good around us. All of us typically adapt to positive things in our lives, and the experiences habituate and become mundane after so much repetition. Even paradise would become tedious after enough time.

The second form of happiness, which should be seen as an addition to the first, rather than a replacement, is living a life of engagement. This involves finding something we love—work, parenting, love, leisure time, and hobbies. As we engage in these activities, we lose ourselves in what many refer to as the zone. In the literature, this is described as "flow"—that place where we feel a sense of inner clarity, focus, concentration, and outside of ordinary reality (Csíkszentmihályi, 1990). We live life as a work of art, rather than as a chaotic response to external events. A life filled with flow experience is likely to be a fulfilling and happy one.

Examples of flow would be gardening, playing music, learning to dance, reading a book or playing a video game. The individuals lose themselves in the activity and they are engaged and focused on what is in front of them. There is an example of this flow stated in Example from the Expert 4.2.

EXAMPLE FROM THE EXPERT— 4.2: FLOW

I often joke with people that I like to do the dishes at home because it gives me a sense of completion in a world fraught with chaos and destruction. I suppose it is one of those jokes that has some truth in it. It's what Stephen King writes in the front material of his bestseller book *IT*, "Fiction is the truth inside the lie." I suppose we all have a bit of truth in our jokes and lies.

Flow experiences require five main things. These are tasks:

1. You are able to focus on
2. That have a clear objective
3. That are challenging, but within your abilities
4. You have the knowledge to complete
5. Where there is feedback on how you are doing.

For me, the dishes are a flow state, a task that I can lose myself in and don't have to think about. I am able to focus on the task at hand. There is a clear objective in front of me. The dishes need to be cleaned, but while doing them is a challenge, the task is within my abilities to complete. I also know when they are done. The pile of dishes moves from point A in the sink to point B in the drying rack. When I am done, there is immediate feedback on the task. I am done because there are no more dirty dishes and they are now clean.

How does this apply to supervision? The good news is we can create a flow state with just about any mundane task. Imagine having to enter hundreds of Excel sheet entries. Simply break the task down into smaller chunks and reward yourself when you finish entering 30 lines of data. Try using color-shaded cells that give you a sense of progress. Go for a walk when you complete each 100 entries. Our minds are powerful tools that have the ability to make a mundane, mind-numbing task into something of a competition. A good supervisor finds creative ways to engage their employees in flow.

At my previous workplace, we used to ring the bell out front each time a clinical staff member had caught up on their notes for the day. This became a kind of fun Pavlovian response the entire office looked forward to and then cheered when one of the staff reached for the bell.

Brian Van Brunt, Ed.D.
The NCHERM Group

The third form of happiness is the highest form and should be seen as further progression from the first two conditions; not replacing them, but building upon them. This third stage of happiness is understanding the meaning of your life. Knowing what your highest strengths are and using them to belong to and join in the service of something larger than you are. It is finding the perfect job where you can be engaged in the everyday, but also give back to others and the larger community.

While it won't be found in any employee handbook, one task a supervisor often has is helping the employee find their passion in their lives. When they are passionate about their work, it moves faster and doesn't feel like work any longer. Tennyson describes this sense of purpose and direction as The Gleam:

"Launch your vessel,
And crowd your canvas,
And, ere it vanishes
Over the margin,
After it, follow it,
Follow The Gleam."
Alfred Lord Tennyson, *Merlin and The Gleam*

67

The positive psychology approach overlaps well the four generations we discuss in the text. The idea of altruism and giving back to a larger cause resonates across the Millennial, Gen X, Boomer and Mature perspectives. The idea of losing oneself in the flow of meaningful work that gives back to the larger community is a shared experience most can appreciate apart from their age and experiences.

DISCUSSION QUESTIONS

1. What are some ways to apply the concepts of Carl Rogers' work to the supervision process? Are there certain departments that would respond better to this approach compared to others? What of the assertion in Example from the Expert 4.1, by Dr. Maria Nieto-Senour, that from a generational perspective we see young people demonstrating behaviors that stand in contrast to our values? How might this play out in your leadership of staff from generations other than your own?

2. Talk about a positive experience you had with a supervisor who was able to convey a sense of genuineness and congruence during your time together. How might you be able to be more genuine and congruent with those you are supervising? Think about some examples of what you can share within the boundaries and limits of the relationship.

3. Over the next week, listen for metaphors in everyday conversation. Look for ways to engage the person in conversation around their metaphor and see if you can use their language to expand their metaphor.

4. What might be some examples of how to apply positive psychology concepts with an employee you are supervising?

5. Discuss how to apply flow theory to some of the mundane, everyday tasks that you have to complete during your workday. There is some food for thought in Example from the Expert 4.2 to encourage your imagination.

Just One Thing

Nola Butler-Byrd, Ph.D., LPCC
Associate Professor, Community-Based Block Program Director
Department of Counseling & School Psychology
College of Education, San Diego State University

As a program director, former department chair and senate committee chair on diversity, as well as a woman of African descent, the one thing I have to keep reminding myself about is to practice daily self-care. My role as a leader is very time- and energy-consuming, and often a very thankless job, that I do because the programs and students that I lead need the power that comes from my leadership. I have often looked up from my laptop or a meeting and realized that I've neglected my needs— even basic needs like eating, running to the lav or exercising, let alone taking the time to "smell the roses."

The presumption of incompetence that faculty of color face in the academy can be very demoralizing and must be tempered with the psychological strengths that Joseph White articulates that support our resilience and brilliance, especially improvisation, a gallows sense of humor and a healthy skepticism about Eurocentric-dominant institutions.

Chapter Five

Know Thyself ...
and Thy Staff

KEY TAKE-A-WAYS

- Self-awareness is a useful first step to becoming the best leader or manager we can be. Gaining an understanding of ourselves as we relate to those around us, understanding our biases and values, and maintaining a keen eye for our blind spots help to position us to better understand our teams.
- Using assessments can be an effective way to bring a common shared language to help build community among teams with diverse generational experience. Two proven assessments that help develop self-awareness and increase understanding among teams are the Gallup StrengthsFinder 2.0 and the Myers-Briggs Type Indicator.
- We all have different preferences when it comes to how we communicate with others. Some of us are extroverted in our interactions while others tend to be introverted. Some of us focus on our feelings when making a decision; others think things through based on facts and figures.

INTRODUCTION

"No one is in control of your happiness but you."

Barbara de Angelis

One of the most central concepts to our development—personally and professionally—is the notion that we alone are in charge of our own happiness. In this context, "happiness" can be read as having a sense of purpose that drives us, our professional fulfillment, and engagement in our work. Leaders and managers understand the challenges of the day-to-day.

There are limitless opportunities to become overworked and overwhelmed—as employees, each of us has had to wrestle with this reality, and as managers and leaders, it is up to us to set positive examples for our staff that demonstrate healthy and positive approaches to our work. Indeed, our leadership and managerial positions present us as *role models* to our staff.

Self-awareness is a useful first step to becoming the best leader or manager we can be. Gaining an understanding of ourselves as we relate to those around us, understanding our biases and values, and maintaining a keen eye for our blind spots help to position us to better understand our teams. This is the first step on the path to leadership practices that will build or strengthen the community within our teams. Self-awareness helps us to both regulate ourselves as we lead teams, as well as demonstrating the importance of self-exploration, growth and development for our multi-generational employees.

But within the context of being a leader who places a primary value on the relationships we have with our staff, how do we even begin to tackle the job of knowing and increasing our understanding of them? In this chapter, we will explore the use of assessments as a tool to increasing our self-knowledge, and our understanding and appreciation for the unique talents, gifts and work styles of our staff. Self-assessments can help clarify the ways that leaders and their teams are different from one another, bringing a broad spectrum of talents and skills to the workplace. They can also clarify the ways they are similar, finding connection and binding points that will foster community within teams. They provide a useful common language for employees to bridge diverse generational experiences in order to understand the ways we are more alike than different and to help position us to capitalize, rather than minimize, one another in the context of our work.

Be a Better Boss

Chances are if you were asked to shut your eyes and think about "*that boss*," it wouldn't take you long to conjure their unwelcome image in your brain. This is the boss who drove you crazy with their micro-managing ways, the one who was overly critical, checked out, or constantly taking your ideas as their own (you know the one). Infusing any conversation on management and leadership with a call back to "that guy" is useful because we can all relate to the kind of boss we don't want to emulate. Conversely, identifying and putting into practice the behaviors of those we admire can be more of a challenge. But, behavior can change. Those who attend to their own development as leaders, those who embrace a willingness to practice self-awareness are best positioned to find and emulate the leaders they admire. And with good reason: According to a 2015 Gallup survey, a bad supervisor is the number one reason people quit their jobs. So, we have a clear motivation to be the best that we can be: *retaining talent for a stronger team and organization.*

INCREASING UNDERSTANDING

Two proven tools to enhance increased understanding and foster community on teams are the Myers-Briggs Type Inventory (MBTI) and the Gallup StrengthsFinder 2.0 Assessment. Businesses, individuals and groups have used these approaches to better understand how we communicate with others around us and make decisions in our personal and professional lives. Managers and leaders using these methods should tread carefully to avoid conveying the idea that they are requiring personality tests for all of their staff or that these measures are being used to label people or put them into boxes. As with any tool, maintaining a keen eye to appropriate application and utilization is critical.

We'll call this the "touchy-feely counseling" warning. Some people approach these kind of reflective questionnaires with excitement and curiosity. The idea of knowing yourself better and learning new ways to understand and communicate with others more effectively can be an attractive prospect. For others, this kind of self-reflective group exercise is analogous to one of the levels of hell in Dante's *Inferno*. The idea of taking an afternoon to fill out the assessment and then discuss its implications within the workplace may not be a pleasant task.

A frank discussion of this elephant in the room prior to engaging in the assessment will help staff feel validated in their hesitations and will support them "getting on board" with the program. In the language of Myers-Briggs, there are likely to be some introverted staff who may not be as comfortable sharing their concerns about the training in an open forum. Here, managers can support staff by providing awareness of the assessment through email or in person prior to the training to allow them time to adjust. Likewise, a manager may need to reduce some of the outspoken enthusiasm from the extroverts in the group. These individuals may "try" to help those not as comfortable sharing, through pressure or intimidation that will be counterproductive.

In the end, we find this kind of self-exploration is a value-add toward the goal of helping improve communication and understanding in the workplace. While there may be an additional cost to administer these measures (and staff may not always like the idea of introspection and reflection), it has been our experience that these exercises pay off in the long run.

EXAMPLE FROM THE EXPERT—
5.1: HOW LEADERS RELATE TO THEIR PEOPLE IS JOB #1

> "People don't care how much you know until they know how
> much you care."
>
> Theodore Roosevelt

I once worked with a leader who could not understand how I knew
so much about her people! What I discovered is that she came into
the side door every morning and up the back staircase to her office. I
came in the front door and talked to the receptionist, walked through
the main work area, said good morning to everyone and stopped and
chatted. In 5–10 minutes I knew who was out of office or had sick
kids, which projects were off budget or timeline, who was pregnant,
and was able to discover the general vibe of the day. I was simply
investing time in people and building relationships through very
small but intentional actions in my day.

I have also worked in environments where the leaders walk right
past their entire teams in the cubes on a daily basis without any
acknowledgement. These leaders were even given direct feedback at
times from their people about how nice it would be if they stopped and
talked. "Get to know me" was the message being sent. The "excuse"
was that they were in a hurry to get to their next meeting and didn't
have time. As human beings, two of our basic needs are having a sense
of belonging and feeling significant in some way—it matters that I'm
here. As a leader, what message is my behavior sending?

When those leaders walked past all of us in our cubes and never said
anything I questioned whether I belonged or mattered. When I can only
communicate in emails and don't have an in-person connection, I know
that you don't know who I am. Emails are for communicating
information, not having a connection. Stopping to deliver a simple
message of "thanks" or "congrats" or "good job" or "hope you are
feeling better today" for a person, greatly enhances how acknowledged
they feel. I've listened to people make up great stories that may or may
not be true when they don't have a relationship with their boss and
something unpleasant happens. We don't give the boss the benefit of the
doubt! We know what we know—which is, "my boss cares about me"
or, "my boss doesn't really care about me at all" or, "I don't matter".

Self-awareness is very important to be a successful leader. Every
action and word is delivering a message to your people of whether

they belong or are significant to you. Where your attention goes and whom your attention goes to is being noticed—and it matters! You will quickly be found out if you have favorites, or if everyone matters and the support of the team is encouraged.

Leaders make all the difference—in how the work gets done, in how their people think and feel about their work, about themselves, and about each other. Leaders influence what employees bring of themselves to work—their heart, their mind, their creativity, their dreams and goals. Those same employees invest themselves into our students. If student success is our goal, then it behoves us to care about the success of our staff, as well!

Think about the jobs you've had; they've been different. Some leaders have inspired you to want to try harder, to be your best? Have you ever had a job where you clearly show up to collect your paycheck? Despite what might be going on in your campus, the team's leader can make all the difference in how people show up, and what work gets accomplished.

In another setting, I worked with a team of 25 who included Millennials to Matures, 25–70 years old. Our leader was so respectful to each of us. She honored and recognized the work of everyone. I never felt the "generational" divide on that team. We were all important. The team worked together developing curriculum and utilizing our different experiences and knowledge. The leader set the stage. We cared about each other, the product we created, and we took care of each other as people. I've had great success building cross-generational cultures of respect and have used tools to assess and understand my team, and to help them understand and relate to one another. The MBTI and StrengthsFinder 2.0 are two such tools, and among my favorites. These inventories serve as a starting point for a conversation. I use those tools with my team to stimulate self-awareness and to learn new ways to understand and communicate. And also to have some laughs at our differences! Thank goodness we aren't all alike!

Taking the time and opportunity to help your employees understand and accept themselves and their strengths and then learn to "flex" your natural style to work with different people makes everyone successful. Using these tools to make "excuses" for my leadership behavior or others is a misuse of the tools. Remember, while assessments are a useful starting point, there is so much more to each individual than his or her personality inventories.

As a leader, I set an intention to create a culture respectful of the diversity of the team, and ensure that I model how to treat others. How do I speak to and about others? What behaviors do I allow to go on in my direct reports, and also the next level down? Do I address the tough issues, or ignore them? Are there behaviors that are unacceptable and I respectfully call those out appropriately, not shaming people in front of others? Am I willing to speak up in tough situations with my boss or my peers?

When an employee knows you care about them and want to help them succeed in their position, as well as in their career and in their life, they will care more about doing a good job and even go the extra mile when necessary. Employees also know if their manager is sincere. People can smell manipulation. Employees respond so positively when they are treated with respect and thoughtfulness; encouraged, appreciated, and even pushed to develop and get out of their comfort zone.

The most effective leaders develop relationships with their people that are genuine and authentic. Getting to know your team members for who they are as people is one of the most important jobs of a leader. And, it's not all work! It's exciting to learn more about where they came from, what excites them, what challenges them, what dreams they have, what beliefs they hold, and where they want to take their career.

There is always more than we might realize about our team members and we do them a service when we get to know them in a way that ensures we are utilizing all of their strengths, experience and knowledge. As a leader, it is my responsibility to mentor my staff to grow in their positions, as well as in their overall careers. And for me, I continue to enjoy mentoring many former staff over many years in their careers. I love watching people accomplish their dreams and do amazing things. As I look back on my career I realize I learned the importance of having a relationship with my staff from one of my first managers. She modeled how to have a professional relationship with me and grow me in my job, and also know me and care about me as a person. I've taken that gift and shared it throughout my career.

Eileen Piersa, M.S., M.A.
Director of Education Operations and Campus Relations
Institute for Palliative Care
Cal State University, San Marcos

THE GALLUP STRENGTHSFINDER 2.0

Gallup StrengthsFinder 2.0 (StrengthsFinder) is a web-based assessment, part of the Gallup StrengthsQuest program, which has foundations in positive psychology. A fundamental starting point is the belief that it is easier to go from good to great than it is to go from mediocre to good. What this means is that individuals should have a clear sense of, and capitalize on, what they do well, and not spend so much time focused on deficits. While we will provide a summary of the assessment here, we leave a more detailed exploration of the research behind the StrengthsFinder assessment to the various books written on the subject (Rath & Conchie, 2009; Rath, 2007; Clifton et al., 2006).

The StrengthsFinder assessment presents the user with 177 items, and organizes and orders the user's capabilities into 34 Talent Themes that fall into 4 Domains of Strength: *Executing*: this hard worker is the person you turn to in order to see solutions implemented; *Influencing*: this individual is the take charge speaker of the house; *Relationship Building*: this individual turns groups into teams and has a talent for getting things done through relationships; and *Strategic Thinking*: this individual takes in and makes sense of information in support of the goals of the team or organization.

Talents are described as "naturally occurring patterns of thought, feeling, or behavior that can be productively applied." The 34 talent themes have names that range from "Empathy"—that are clearly understood and a part of our day-to-day vernacular—to "WOO," short for "winning others over," that have been developed as a part of the program's unique language (Clifton et al., 2006). Users receive their top five StrengthsFinder talent themes report, organizing information to help them not only better understand their unique talents and talent combinations, but also to provide the user with language to clearly and succinctly describe their talents to others. In the land of self-knowledge and discovery, this can be a powerful tool for understanding and sharing one's gifts.

What is important to understand about the StrengthsFinder is not that it is most advantageous for an individual to have talents represented across the four domains, but that it is key to having talents in each domain represented throughout our teams. In the land of Strengths, this is the most effective way to ensure that leaders are able to leverage the strength of their teams and help their members put their strengths to work each day.

PUTTING YOUR STRENGTHS TO WORK AS A LEADER

In their book, *Strengths Based Leadership*, Tom Rath and Barry Conchie explore what they describe as three keys to effective leadership:

1. The knowledge of your own strengths and an investment in the strengths of those around you.
2. The assembling of teams that reflect the strengths necessary for the job at hand.
3. The awareness of and responsiveness to the basic needs of those you lead.

This means first knowing your own strengths, and second, a willingness to take an interest in and put to work the strengths of your team members. Sounds like the perfect job for StrengthsFinder 2.0!

EXAMPLE FROM THE EXPERT—
5.2: MY STRENGTHS REVOLUTION

It was a few semesters into graduate school, far enough that expectations were more clear and classmates were more aware of each other's differences. As the classmates were settling in and chatting about their days, what was new in life and the semester starting, in walked the professor. Nobody knew him, although we had heard of him through other classmates from prior cohorts or coworkers. I'll never forget the awkward start of that class as some classmates appeared as though the sky was falling when no syllabus was presented on the first night to set clear expectations and others were enamored by the warm, eccentric professor. The course was a required graduate level counseling course for students in a higher education program, so we were going to stick with it regardless of personality types.

As the class progressed and the professor produced a syllabus—to the indifference of some and to please others—which he made clear as he passed it out, I found myself in the "indifferent" category. I was there because I had to be, I was going to make the most of it as I cared about student development and knew counseling had a significant role in that. In addition, I had no judgments about the professor or either group of students. What I didn't know or expect is what transpired over the next couple semesters and into the last 15 years of my professional and personal life.

I recall "Chip," as he preferred to be called, coming into class early on with colored plastic sunglasses, and I shared his analogy about seeing life through various lenses. He was passionate about helping students achieve their greatest potential by understanding their natural talents. I will never forget him asking us to read a draft of

77

a book he was working on with an organization I knew very little about at the time. This book, *StrengthsQuest*, became a game changer in education, taking what the late Donald Clifton of The Gallup Organization had learned about peoples' strengths in the world of work and applying it to student development to, as Chip Anderson would say, "develop whole students."

During graduate school the cohort had two courses with Chip and at work we were using strengths in the first year experience program, so I was becoming a solid believer in Chip's ideas around use of strengths in student development. I began putting it to practice coaching students in all aspects of life including career planning. What I didn't know at the beginning of that class was that I was embarking on a revolution, and even those who were disgruntled at the commencing of the semester had a life-changing experience. We were touched by the late Chip Anderson and the "Strengths Revolution," as Chip liked to call it. When I transitioned from Azusa Pacific to take an opportunity at a large community college district, Chip asked as he hugged me goodbye that I help him continue the "strengths revolution" in the community college. The next year Chip Anderson lost a battle with cancer, but his legacy lived on and was spreading across borders. He had touched lives who began to evangelize others and help continue the work he and Don had started.

After Chip's passing, I had begun training other educators in the use of StrengthsQuest and found it particularly useful when managing additional staff from diverse backgrounds. Because of what I hadlearned, I was able to use my talents of Individualization and Maximizer to see the potential in employees others did not see. As I worked with these struggling employees, helping them to see their own potential, they began applying their talents in new ways within their roles and soon became sought-after team members, recruited to other departments throughout the institution. Capitalizing on my Futuristic, Individualization, Maximizer, Relator and Achiever themes, I was able to take community college departments from a road to despair to a new level of success by catching and casting a clear vision of the future, identifying the right talent for the job, and recognizing the potential to take good to great while building meaningful work relationships that would positively affect not only the organization, but the students that came through our doors every day.

Every educator has the opportunity to have a similar impact on students, alumni, faculty and staff. Whether through the use of the StrengthsFinder assessment, or simply by helping people recognize and capitalize on their strengths, we can continue the legacy of the strengths revolution. It's a matter of how we look at people, recognizing that it is time to look at what is right with people instead of trying to fix what is wrong with people. Focusing on students' and employees' innate talents helps them to reach their greatest potential.

Ron Gaschler
Associate Director, Career Services
University of Arizona

EXAMPLE FROM THE EXPERT— 5.3: PUTTING STRENGTHS TO WORK

As I walked out of the one-on-one meeting with her, I was beyond aggravated. I wasn't sure if I wanted to go into my office and cry or to head down to our Human Resource office and start the paperwork to have her fired. Three months after having been promoted from peer to manager, my relationship with one of my employees was clearly strained. I couldn't understand why she was so resistant to any of my advice or guidance. Her performance was average, not superior but certainly not anything that justified removing her fromher role. Her interpersonal behavior with the rest of our team, however, was offensive. She was off-putting in meetings, cold to her fellow team members and aggressive in her pushback to what I was trying to do with our team.

Taking the advice of a mentor, I set up a series of one-on-one conversations with her in hopes of building a stronger personal relationship and trying to provide some constructive feedback on how her actions were affecting the rest of the team. These meetings produced little fruit and this most recent conversation ended with her standing across a table, pointing her finger in my face and yelling at me about what a terrible leader I was and how she had no respect for anything I was trying to do. As she stormed out of the room I was hurt, angry and at a loss for what to do next.

Sitting at my desk later that evening preparing for a team-building exercise for an upcoming retreat, I was reviewing the Gallup StrengthsFinder results for my team. I noticed the team had a remarkable amount of consistent themes—Empathy, Harmony, Relator, Achiever, Input, Learner—with the exception of one employee who had themes not shared by the rest of the team: Command, Self-Assurance, Ideation, Activator & Focus. I knew instantly who this employee was without even looking at the name on the report! As I pored over her unique Signature Talent Themes, I began to understand more of what drove the passion, actions and perspective of this team member. As I learned about these talent themes I began to realize that the approach I was taking to lead her was completely misguided based on her strengths. I was unintentionally ignoring her strengths and asking her to work out of a place of non-talent. It was no wonder she was so frustrated with me. In a deeply humbling moment I realized that by not honoring this person's strengths, I was partially responsible for creating this strained relationship.

A week later I took a very different approach with this team member; I opened the meeting by telling her about a procedural problem facing our team and told her that I thought she would be a good person to help us find a solution. I asked her to be in charge of this project, owning the entire process of researching the issue and brainstorming a series of potential solutions and asked for her to report back in two weeks on her findings. As I was describing this project to her, I watched as she fought against an enormous smile that was creeping across her face; she was elated, she just didn't want me to know.

She handled the project better than I had expected. She made a presentation to the rest of the team about how she had come up with a solution to reduce a problem in the department. The team then began to see her more a peer.

While my relationship with this team member was never strong, it became productive and effective when I took a strengths-based approach. More importantly, I learned one of the most valuable leadership lessons in my professional career; leaders must lead people from a place of their strengths. Leaders don't have one leadership style; instead, they have as many unique styles of leadership as the number of people they are seeking to lead. Each person has a unique set of strengths and they are most engaged and effective when they are set free to do what they do best.

Kyle Robinson
Higher Education Consultant,
formerly of the Gallup Organization

THE MYERS-BRIGGS TYPE PERSONALITY INDICATOR

We all have different preferences when it comes to how we communicate with others. Some tend towards extroversion, others towards introversion; some focus on feelings when decision-making, for others decisions are more facts-and-figures based. There are several brief measures useful to determine a person's preferences when it comes to their personality style and how they communicate. These include the Myers-Briggs Type Indicator (www.myersbriggs.org) and the Keirsey Temperament Sorter (www.keirsey.com). These may be helpful to give and to better identify preferences. It may be that a university's career counseling unit has access to these tests.

Much has been written on the Myers-Briggs Type Indicator (MBTI) in terms of the four different two-directional scales and the sixteen possible permutations of these characteristics. We summarize the eight categories here, but leave a more detailed exploration of the MBTI types to various books written on the subject (Keirsey, 1998; Hirsch & Kummerow, 1989; Thomson, 1998; Kroeger & Thuesen, 1988; Keirsey & Bates, 1978). It's worth clarifying that those taking the MBTI often find their preferences are not static and change over time. Additionally, the following eight (paired) categories are best seen on a continuum. For example, it is rare to have someone who is completely extroverted, but more common to have a tendency towards extroversion over introversion. Seeing these as a range or a spectrum is helpful.

Another way to see the following categories is to understand that these are our preferences for interaction, decision-making or making sense of the world. These are the ways we find ourselves recharged and ready to take on a new day. So it is important to understand that just because someone is introverted doesn't mean they can't be social at parties when required. Similarly, someone who is typically sensing can also take a break from the here-and-now data to demonstrate intuition during a task they have become familiar with over time.

Introversion vs. Extroversion

Where does the person get their energy? Where do they prefer to focus their attention? Introverts prefer to focus on their inner world and are more comfortable with introspection and not social interactions. Introverts tend to think things out in detail before acting and like to understand things before experiencing them. Extroverts are energized by social interaction with others and prefer to communicate through talking and experience. They are action oriented and are focused on the outer world and the environment.

A person who leans toward introversion will be more comfortable in the workplace working independently, reflecting on the nature of the project. They are careful and cautious before acting. This may cause them to lose opportunities to act. They may also struggle with relationships with others and may be seen as secretive or misunderstood. A person who leans towards extroversion is often seen as open and interacts well with others around them. They thrive on change and may be seen as impulsive or impatient with office rules and routine.

Sensing vs. Intuition

How does the person see the world? How do they acquire new information? Sensing individuals live in the here and now and appreciate the realities of a situation. They are described as realistic and practical. Sensing individuals focus on the trees instead of the forest. Intuitive people look at the big picture and find meaning in relationships and possibilities beyond their senses. They value imagination and can see the possibilities and value of new ways of doing things.

A person who approaches the world from a sensing viewpoint has a good attention to detail and is focused on facts and is seen as patient by others. A sensing person may become frustrated with complex projects and may become overwhelmed with too many or competing facts. They have trouble trusting their instincts on projects in the absence of facts. This is in contrast to intuitive-leaning individuals; here they are seeing the possibilities and are charged by new ideas. They enjoy solving complicated and novel problems. Intuitive individuals may have trouble attending to specific detail and can become impatient with tedious assignments. They have a tendency to jump to conclusions.

Thinking vs. Feeling

What is the preferred method to make decisions? Those who value thinking are described as logical and objective and seek an objective standard of truth; a sense of right and wrong. Thinkers weigh the evidence and analyze what is wrong. A feeling person is focused on what is important to themselves and others and makes decisions on these values. They decide based on how much you care or what kind of personal investment you have. They operate with tact and sympathy.

An individual focused on thinking comes across as logical, analytical and objective. They are seen as just and are able to stand firm on their beliefs. Given this internal focus, they may not always be tuned in to other people's feelings and, as a result, may misunderstand those feelings. They do not show their feelings and are generally uninterested in persuading others to their perspective or showing mercy toward other perspectives or behaviors. A feeling person first considers the needs and values of others, shares their own feelings and may seek to persuade and arouse others. They tend to be less organized and are not governed by logic or objective facts. When they make a judgment it is often based on feelings rather than logic.

Judging vs. Perceiving

How does the person structure their world? How do they orient themselves to the outer world? A judging person lives in a very orderly and planned way in an attempt to regulate and control life. They desire things to come to a close and value the settling of things and the ability to move on with what is next. A perceiving person is more flexible and spontaneous and trusts their ability to adapt. They are open to what life brings and like to gather information and keep their options open. They have a desire to understand rather than to control.

A judging person focuses on the task. They make quick decisions and can be seen as stubborn or inflexible. They may make decisions with incomplete data, are focused on the plan and don't tolerate being interrupted well. A perceptive person has little focus on planning and often can be seen as indecisive. They are able to see all sides of an issue, can be flexible and don't come across as judgmental. They can be easily distracted from tasks and do not finish projects well.

We remind you of Professor Snape's famous introduction to the potions class from the *Harry Potter* book series, "You are here to learn the subtle science and exact art of potion-making." There have been several negative articles about the accuracy of the MBTI and similar measures in terms of their validity and the consistency of the individual characteristics over time. However, it has been our experience that the MBTI creates opportunities to explore differences, improve understanding among team members, and prepares managers to better anticipate and get out ahead of potential conflicts or difficulties when it comes to decision-making and project completion. As with any tool, or wizard-making potion class— application is more successful with an appreciation for both the science and art of the tool and process.

EXAMPLE FROM THE EXPERT— 5.4: RED CARS AND EPCOT

OK, I get it. It's an odd title for this brief reflection. But hang in there with me ...

When I was younger in my professional career, I had several supervisors who administered the MBTI to me as part of our work. Later in my clinical practice, I found myself administering and using the Myers-Briggs and similar inventories to explore personality differences and how individuals communicate.

On the MBTI, my ratings came up as ENFP. This makes me an extroverted, intuitive, feeling- and perception-oriented person. My wife also took the MBTI and we found that her score was the exact opposite of mine at ISTJ. This makes her an introvert, sensing, thinking- and judgment-oriented person. And let's not forget the Internet quizzes: I'm Eowyn in *Lord of the Rings*, Luna Lovegood in *Harry Potter* and Qui-Gon Jinn in *Star Wars*. She's Elrond in *Lord of the Rings*, Draco Malfoy in *Harry Potter* and Darth Vader in *Star Wars*. A recipe for disaster and divorce, right? Well, maybe not. At least according to MC Skat Kat and Paula Abdul's song *Opposites Attract*.

What the MBTI taught us was the importance of appreciating our differences and finding ways to complement each other, rather than escalating the friction of our differences. For example, we learnedthat the way I approach buying a car is finding the pretty red one that goes really fast. Her approach is to research things like safety, maintenance history and re-sale value. In the end, we are stronger when we work together leaning on our strengths. And yes, I realize I'm pushing the concept of 'strength' when I suggest wanting a red sports car as an example.

When we travel together to Walt Disney World, my ideal vacation is to get a margarita, buy one of those sombreros from EPCOT's Mexico and drink my way over to lunch in Germany. I alternate this with spending time in the lazy river at Blizzard Beach or catching a wave at Typhoon Lagoon. Her idea of a good Walt Disney World vacation is to break out the Excel sheet and plan our meals and fast-passes throughout the trip. She signs up for tours, reads lengthy review books and has an app on her phone so that she can get real-time updates on-line for wait times.

We have a better vacation when we understand how each of us approaches our ideal area and we find opportunities to compromise and lean into each other's strengths. She brings her Kindle and finds a quiet, shady spot by the pool since unstructured floating with groups of random strangers isn't her thing. I get the better part of the deal because her planning and organization helps us go on more rides and have reservations (seriously, six months out?) at some of the better restaurants.

When looking at measuring employees' attitudes towards communication and change, homogeneity shouldn't be our departmental goal. Instead, I've found that offices I've had the privilege to oversee have worked better when it came to having diversity in our MBTI or StrengthsFinder. The key, as with many things, is the importance of understanding how others approach problems and communication when you interact with them on projects, in supervision, or in providing service to students.

Also, I currently have a red Camaro and take the lead on chatting people up for us in social outings. She does all of our vacation planning and keeps our checkbook. She has the patience to put up with me and I have the grace and humility to know that I got the better part of this deal... despite her occasional retreat into her hamster-ball of quiet and isolated space.

Brian Van Brunt, Ed.D.
The NCHERM Group

Whether you are comfortable using measures such as StrengthsFinder or the MBTI with your employees, or are more at ease with simply exploring informally their preferences for making decisions, approaching work, processing through conflict or being part of a social community, the lesson of this chapter is found in the importance of managers and leadership developing a better understanding of themselves and of their workforce. This is an investment we call upstream work: addressing problems at source in an attempt to smooth operations during times of increased productivity and potential frustration or stress. When we have a better understanding of our employees' preferences (and our employees' understanding of ours!) we create a more streamlined and success-oriented workplace.

EXAMPLE FROM THE EXPERT—
5.5: LEARNING AND LIVING YOUR STRENGTHS

The Career Services office at my current institution has in their mission statement to help students, to "discover, develop, and apply their unique talents." The moment I read this mission statement, it resonated with me. I yearned to go back in time to my twenties in order to be supported in my own time of discovery and development. Having aged out of the foster care system, I had very little exposure to career exploration—and I sure didn't have any idea what my strengths were.

After some years in the work world, I had formed a script that went something like this: "If that's what it takes to be a leader, I'll never be a leader." The "it" in that statement was what I saw exemplified in leadership: a cold aloofness and an apparent disconnection from the "people side" of the office. It seemed to me that my inclination to tear up at work would be a barrier to my long-term success. I was, as I told myself, just *too sensitive.*

This was my story, and I was most definitely sticking to it.

After a time, I completed my undergrad degree and settled into a direct service position working as a Disability Specialist at a community college. I liked working with students because, owing to my sensitive nature, I saw my strengths in being an advocate on behalf of students with disabilities. Several years into this role, an (angel in the form of) Interim Dean, Gene Morones, gently told me that I was burnt out—that I needed to go back to school to get my Masters so that I could move up professionally and begin running the office I'd contributed to for so long. As I reflect back on this conversation, I realize how special it was. As an Interim Dean, he might not have noticed my burnout, he might not have cared to encourage my growth... but he did both!

I applied and was accepted to San Diego State University, and there I engaged in an innovative program with an emphasis on training multiculturally competent counselors, skilled at working with multi-ethnic, socioeconomically diverse clients. As a student, I was actively involved in structuring the learning experience and explored issues including sexism, racism, poverty, and disability, and their implications. As a non-traditional student, I noticed how much my age "mattered" in the classroom—I brought experiences that younger students hadn't yet had. I could see, for example, very clearly how being aware of the developmental place of our clients would make a difference to the clinician–client dynamic. I did not yet realize how frequently I would use this knowledge when working with the staff I would later lead.

One day in a cohort meeting, tears welled in my eyes as I listened to a fellow student share her painful experience. Later, I shared with Dr. Maria Nieto-Senour, Faculty and Program Director, that because I was "always in tears," I would never be a great clinician or leader of people. She thought for a moment before replying to me. "I don't experience you that way," she said. "Always in tears?" was her question to me. I had to push against that story I carried of myself. "Well," I replied, "I guess I should say, I have tears close to the surface," struggling to find the right words. "I feel what other people feel, and it holds me back." Maria smiled gently and said, "Kiddo, that is what will make you a great counselor, a great leader."

A new narrative

This conversation with Maria was the first time that my high empathy was presented to me as a strength. I'd certainly never seen it that way, and the stories others told about my sensitivity were rarely ever positive. Later, when I was exposed to the Gallup StrengthsFinder assessment, I was not surprised to read my report and find Empathy as my top strength. By then, I had begun to see myself in a new way, and to tell a new story about my talents. I learned that I could beeffective working with students, staff and colleagues by putting my strengths to work, and putting myself in their shoes.

I learned that I could be an effective leader, not *in spite of* my high empathy, but *because* of it.

After I completed my graduate degree, I knew the time had come for me to leave the community college that I loved in order to foster my growth. I felt confident I could take on a new challenge where leadership would be a part of my job. I was offered a position that would allow me to put my strengths and experience to work establishing the disability services office of my current institution.

I share this story of Gene and Maria, and their impact on me, because they highlight three critical elements to effective leaders:

1. They care about our growth and development.
2. They will take on difficult conversations in order to effect positive change.
3. They have a unique power to help us to re-author the stories that hold us back and to help us uncover our strengths.

Poppy Fitch, M.A.
Associate Vice President, Student Affairs
Ashford University

DISCUSSION QUESTIONS

1. Why is self-awareness important to being an effective leader or manager? How do I measure my effectiveness as a leader or manager? How can assessments help me to know more about myself as a leader or manager?
2. Are my values about what it means to be a good manager or effective leader consistent with the values of the team(s) that I lead? How can I check this out?
3. In what ways can I utilize assessments to increase understanding across my team(s)? Are there non-formal mechanisms I can use in order to identify and capitalize on the strengths of my team members?
4. What barriers to success may exist when using assessments in the workplace?
5. Will my employees of different generations experience the use of assessments similarly?

Just One Thing

Greg Elliott, M.A., LPC
Director, Counseling & Career Services
Adams State University

Hire to maximize diversity, not to surround yourself with people just like you. As a clinical supervisor of Counseling students and the Director of Counseling & Career Services at Adams State University, it's always been my goal to support my practicum and internship students and full-time staff in developing into the best counselors they can be; not to develop them into copies of myself. The Counseling Center is stronger when we have counselors practicing CBT, Brief Solution-Focused, Existential, Gestalt, Feminist, Reality Therapy, and a diverse array of other perspectives, just as it's stronger when it's staffed with counselors who represent a mix of GLBT, straight, Christian, non-Christian, female, male and all sorts of different races.

As a manager and leader, it's been important for me to do enough self-reflection on my own personal style, and on the feedback I've received from others, to be able to hire people who have different strengths than I do. For example, I perceive one of my own strengths to be my organizational and planning skills; on the Myers-Briggs Type Indicator I'm reflected as a J. But I've found that I enjoy my job much more and we do better work on campus when I intentionally hire employees with a strong P preference. Their spontaneity creates a nice balance to my organizational skills. A diverse staff also helps to break down barriers and stigma that students may face in accessing our services.

Sting once memorably said that "history will teach us nothing," but the idea of promoting and celebrating diversity is not a new one. The United States is a country that was founded on acceptance and integration of a diverse citizenry and on being a country where intelligence and creativity could be the foundation for any individual person to rise to great heights. My department is stronger and our work delivers a greater impact on campus when my staff represents diversity in therapeutic orientation, race, gender, sexual identity and preference, religion, ethnicity, and able-bodiedness.

89

Chapter Six

Team Building and Professional Development
Investing in the Future

KEY TAKE-A-WAYS

- Good investments take planning and effort. Leaders and managers need to carve out time to accomplish these times of reflection and growth in order to invest in the team. Staff retreats, growth exercises and improving communication doesn't happen by accident.
- Management can't just be about addressing negative behaviors. Good managers, leaders and supervisors spend time looking for and acknowledging gold-star moments. Taking the time to identify and praise good work shapes positive behavior and fosters growth, productivity and better attitudes.
- Effective staff development occurs when leadership and management model an excitement and passion for developing team communication, problem-solving and goal focus. When a leader or manager does not value staff retreats or reflective opportunities for growth, neither will their employees.

INTRODUCTION

> "Almost everything will work again if you unplug it for a few minutes, including you."
>
> Anne Lamott

There is little debate over the effectiveness of time away. Whether planning team building for fun or for professional development, an interesting inverse relationship exists that goes something like this: *the more you and your staff need the time, the less energy and wherewithal you possess to plan and execute.* Resonate?

Other barriers exist to prioritizing time for professional development and team building: lack of staff engagement resulting from reduced resources, vacant positions, or a generally disengaged team member who is "poisoning the well." One such barrier that we hear a lot about is the notion that professional development concepts do not always take hold. A wise colleague once said, "If only 1 in 10 concepts resonate and have a lasting impact, then you must keep planning—throw it against the wall and revel in what *does* work!" This is why planning just one professional development activity per year is sub-par... at that rate, you and your team could potentially be waiting ten years for the magic bullet!

For some, team building feels awkward or painful. It's as if the sum total of a team's fun time together is equal to the monthly birthday celebration potluck—that is akin to pulling teeth just to garner the potluck dishes. Tense relationships among team members, frustration over workload, and even just subtle cues that laughter and celebration have no place in your department may be to blame. Some leaders and managers understand this to be a reality on their teams, but are unsure how to even begin to address the issue. And, because it's "just a potluck," they may be inclined to do nothing at all.

WHY IS TEAM BUILDING AND PROFESSIONAL DEVELOPMENT IMPORTANT?

There is science behind the importance of getting your team away from their desks and out of the conference room. Scientist George Gallup and Psychologist Donald Clifton joined forces in 1988, bringing together decades of their individual research on survey and polling technology, and on progressive management science, respectively. One notable result was the Gallup Q12, a survey tool measuring employee engagement. The Q12 consists of 12 items that measure workplace engagement. How important is team building and professional development? Four of the twelve survey items on the Q12 relate to themes around professional development and friendship/camaraderie in the workplace (Harter et al., 2008).

By creating opportunities for our teams to learn and enjoy one another, we set the stage for the creation of a community. McKnight describes *"the culture of community...is something you cannot buy... A culture is the creation of people who are seriously related to each other. It takes time because serious relationships are based upon trust, and trust grows from the experience of being together in a way that makes a difference in our lives."* (2008, p. 2)

Consider Google, number 1 on Fortune's 100 Best Places to Work list. Their innovative and employee-centered approach to the contemporary workplace lavishes perks from free food to generous parenting leaves. These forward thinkers were early and eager responders to their Millennial staff's wish for work–life balance and fun in the workplace. But is this new brand of workplace actually a result of Millennial demands?

Think back to the late nineties, grunge rock and Ally McBeal, a simpler time before the National Security Administration and "liquids and laptops out!" It was in this decidedly Gen X coming of age period that the workplace program *Fish!* emerged. Based upon the roaring success of Seattle's Pike Place Fish Market making work fun by throwing fish at one another, *Fish! A Remarkable Way to Boost Morale and Improve Results* brought a simple epithet to work as a way to impact organizational culture:

1. Choosing one's attitude
2. Playing at work
3. Making someone's day, and …
4. Being present.

These forward thinkers were responding to the Gen Xer entry into the workforce and their desire for fun! What both these examples demonstrate is surely a response to the combined demands of Gen Xer's and Millennials, who all tolled a whopping 68% of the workforce (Fry, 2015).

EXAMPLE FROM THE EXPERT—
6.1: WALKIN' ON SUNSHINE: A TEAM BUILDING POWERHOUSE

Every team has their moments. The Sunshine Club was born when our department was at a low point. Budget reductions and organizational restructuring had strained our once highly engaged team, and we knew something had to change. This team of staff and department leadership came together with one clear and common objective in mind: celebration and laughter.

One of the events universally agreed as a crowning achievement of the Sunshine Club was the 2014 Halloween Potluck. Rather than making this a team or department-wide event, the potluck was open to the departments that shared our workspace including Library Services, the Writing Center, and the Registrar's Office, and was designed to foster friendship and camaraderie between our departments. Not only was the potluck a success, it also directly led to an educational outreach event that was later attended by hundreds of University staff and faculty.

What started as an idea in a Sunshine Club monthly meeting quickly gathered steam. Ideas bounced off of the walls of cubicles as the larger team was brought in to discuss where we wanted to take our Potluck, thematically speaking. There would, of course, be costumes, but it wasn't until one of our counselors recommended that we dress as camp counselors that the event really started to take shape. Costumes were planned. Roles were assigned: one person would be the camp lifeguard, another the nurse, there would be a field guide, and camp cafeteria workers, too. Everyone had the opportunity to take the t-shirts that we had printed (with logos illustrating the office's emphasis on *ability*, rather than disability), and incorporate their unique role and persona into their costume.

It was when we started exploring these roles that our camp name and mantra were born. We were all counselors, and all proud to bring our unique gifts to our own summer camp, Camp CanDo. With the Sunshine Club designing the event, we knew that our Halloween would be more of a treat than a trick.

That morning, our counselors each showed up in their costumes. Our field guide swiped at invisible butterflies with his net, our lifeguard's nose glowed with zinc, our camp nurse donned her stethoscope and checked some unsuspecting colleague's heartbeat. We filed happily into a conference room shouting our camp motto as we walked in line, "Who can? We can! CAMP CANDO!"

As we mingled with the colleagues, friends new and old, we sampled the fare that everyone was all too eager to advertise. "You HAVE to try my barbecue chicken!", "I brought my world-famous cheesy-rice!", "These brownies are my grandmother's secret recipe!" Bread was broken, fingers were licked, and all in attendance marveled at the hard work of the Sunshine Club.

They had transformed the room, and they had done it in under an hour.

The walls were lined with construction paper bats, cobwebs hung thick from a Halloween tree, a skeleton hung silent on the wall, smoke poured from a cauldron of dry ice, steaming over the backpacks, hiking boots, water-skis, and other camp-related props the counselors had brought in. A spooktacular playlist filled the room with horror-themed hits like "Monster Mash" and "Dead Man's

Curve", and monster movies played silently in the background to further set the mood. The party continued as University leadership visited our campsite. They had announced a costume contest weeks in advance, and they laughed and sampled our dishes as we recited our camp chant for them. It came as no surprise when Camp CanDo was later announced the winner of the costume contest.

Being proclaimed the winners isn't the only thing that came out of this effort. The Access and Wellness team took Camp CanDo on the road for an open-house event that spring. Costumes were dusted off, new props were dreamt up, and another, even larger, conference room was turned into our campsite. The day of the open-house, our office shared information about the many accommodations and services we offered to our students. Games were played, prizes awarded, and at the end of the event our building was full of s'more treats, and happy campers.

While it's impossible to measure the impact that the Sunshine Club had on our morale, one of the team's members perhaps summed it up best when she said, "I feel the impact this group had on our team was the ability to feel special, appreciated, and acknowledged. Whether we celebrated birthdays, achievements, life events, or holidays, our team members received individual attention. I think the feeling knowing someone took the time to celebrate you uniquely can add value to us as individuals, and to the culture of the department."

One thing is certain, on days when the Sunshine Club was in action, people were smiling, mouths were watering, rooms were decorated, and the mood around the office just seemed, well... brighter.

With very special thanks to Sam Harvey and the Sunshine Club players:

Carmel Hernandez, Victoria Iyamba, Beth Lund, Katie Tewes, Shaylah Turk & Liz Wilke.

Poppy Fitch, M.A.
Associate Vice President, Student Affairs
Ashford University

A FLY IN THE SOUP

There is that old saying by Henry Ford, "Whether you think you can, or you think you can't—you're right." Planning staff retreats or opportunities for professional development first requires buy-in from senior leadership to be successful. A director or supervisor who negatively comments about department-wide training initiatives, or complains that professional development takes people away from the front-line work the department needs to accomplish, essentially puts a fly in an otherwise appetizing soup—or in a glass of Chardonnay, if you are like the authors and fans of Alanis Morissette (we will, however, avoid a lengthier discussion of the validity of the song *Ironic* where this reference come from).

When director, leader, manager or supervisor fails to support a staff training, retreat or development opportunity, they communicate a meta-communication to their team, "This isn't important to me, so it doesn't have to be important to you." When people do show up for these events, they are distracted, checking their emails and texts on their phones or working on other projects rather than attending to the task at hand. It would be better to not have these events if the people attending don't want to be there or aren't focused on the task at hand.

There are personality tests, communication exercises and group awareness trainings that can overcome a lack of top-down support for these events. In much the same way, the taste or effort that went into cooking the soup in question becomes moot when a fly lands in the middle of it. Those in leadership positions must first lead by example, and there is no better way to accomplish this than showing enthusiasm, support, interest and curiosity for professional development opportunities. These are not things that we *have* to do, they are instead things that we *get* to do.

So what stance do we take when it comes to creating and implementing these types of events and trainings? There are two schools of thought. The first stresses the importance of obtaining buy-in and support from those who will be attending the training. Training and development opportunities tend to be more effective when the people going through the experience have a voice when it comes time to choose the event in question. This provides those charged with leading the event the opportunity to seek input and obtain help in the planning and creation stages, and can create a more contiguous opportunity for all staff to join in and participate. If the content of the training is more complicated or fixed, it may be easier to allow staff input on other ideas such as the food, location or timing of the event.

The second school of thought involves a charismatic leader or manager choosing the training and bringing everyone on board quickly by the sheer power of their enthusiasm and excitement. Bringing in an outside motivational speaker, choosing a program developed by a third-party company, offers an element of surprise that can also be an effective way to keep people excited and engaged in an event.

However, whether the event is a surprise the leader has organized, or something developed more through a grass-roots effort, the idea of buy-in from upper management is essential. Perhaps some of the best professional development and training events are those that alternate between these two schools of thought. The leadership and management plan one event in the spring while the staff vote on and plan the second training event for the fall.

EXAMPLE FROM THE EXPERT— 6.2: PROFESSIONAL DEVELOPMENT PAYS DIVIDENDS

For many, a future investment is a one-time deal. You put something in, and then you wait to watch it grow into something more. But when it comes to our Career and Alumni Service team, a one-time deal just isn't enough. Instead, we believe that continuous professional development leads to even better results. Although we have many priorities to balance, our Career Services Department has remained steadfast in our commitment to continue to develop ourselves as even better career coaches and leaders in the industry. Every two weeks, we commit some time to the professional development of our team members. Our staff takes turns leading discussions and activities around industry trends, troubleshooting difficult situations, role playing, and exploration around the various careers our students may be interested in.

One spring quarter, we decided to utilize our bi-weekly professional development time to read and discuss a career exploration and job search book for graduating college students. We started a book club! The conversations throughout our book club provided us with new language and new activities to try with our students beyond the normal extent of exploring careers through online databases, providing resume critique, and helping in preparing for interviews. But what helped make this book club particularly successful was the way that we shared the responsibility for it. Alternating team members led discussion for different chapters, and had the freedom to guide the discussion or activity in whatever way they wanted. This opened up impressive creativity, and members ultimately walked away with a richer experience.

In fact, the number of new ideas for our practice that arose in these meetings led to a spinoff group that used the ideas in the book to design and implement new resources and guides for the team to integrate into their daily practice with students. Now our office is equipped with new activities, resources, and alternative approaches to coaching—all thanks to our book club! Our conversations are more robust, our options for supporting students are more varied and creative, and our overall level of coaching has improved.

Even a year down the road, we continue to see the payoff from this investment surface in a variety of ways. We recently hosted a Career and Alumni Services Open House, hoping to introduce our department and give our university colleagues a more in-depth view of all services we offer to students and alumni. To pull off a successful event, we worked as one unit for high-level decisions and then relied on the individual strengths of team members to accomplish specific tasks and goals. After a group brainstorm and identifying the desired program outcomes, we had a clear roadmap of where we needed to go from there. Again, allowing individual team members to take the reins really opened up the creativity in the planning process. The one item we noticed that drew a crowd and made a learning experience more fun was developing a theme and creating engaging activities. We decided on the theme of *The Game of Life*; we thought it was a perfect theme for a department that works to improve people's lives.

The remaining details and logistics were divided among the team, and this is where that continual investment comes in. When you put into your team constantly, you have built up the trust needed to truly delegate effectively! So those team members with a bit more clout worked on finding a date and communicating with key stakeholders; our Employer Relations and Alumni folks reached out to employers and local businesses to secure prize donations; others took on more detailed tasks like creating checklists and scheduling necessary meetings and activities leading up to the event. We advertised throughout campus, through a calendar invite, and even printed stickers for the sleeves of the coffee cups at the coffee cart. The "party planners" in the group led the charge of getting people excited with themed décor, prizes, opportunities to compete to win, and a raffle. We took great care in setting up the room to make it similar to *The Game of Life*, and translating it to Career and Alumni Services. We utilized the Career Development Process as a guide to the types of tables and activities we offered at the event.

And this is where the investment comes full circle. To encourage participants to visit each table, team members created poster boards with interactive activities to help people understand how we work with students. More than anything, it was the creative approach to learning that stood out. This was a new way of presenting information for our team, and we were getting pretty good at it! It wasn't simply the book club, or the resources built from that. Rather, such creative performance comes from the consistent investment in the staff. One time isn't enough. Because we had integrated the idea of professional growth in our team, each team member felt empowered to think outside of the box, find new ways to solve problems, and explore how we can better engage others in our process. So, for a real payoff in the end, be sure to *diversify* your investment and *add to it* often.

Tamara Small
Career Services Manager, Ashford University

Sara Headden
Job Developer/Internship Coordinator, San Diego City College

Genesis Lastrella-Quicho
Career Services Specialist, Ashford University

FINDING A PATH FORWARD: SERVANT LEADERSHIP

The heart of the servant leadership movement is the concept that people respond more effectively to ideas and work when they feel they aren't being asked to do anything that the leader, manager or director isn't willing to do themselves. The phrase servant leadership was first used by Robert K. Greenleaf in *The Servant as Leader*, an essay he first published in the 1970s.

Greenleaf (1977) writes, "The idea of the servant as leader came out of reading Hermann Hesse's *Journey to the East*. In this story we see a band of men on a mythical journey, probably also Hesse's own journey. The central figure of the story is Leo who accompanies the party as the servant who does their menial chores, but who also sustains them with his spirit and his song. He is a person of extraordinary presence. All goes well until Leo disappears. Then the group falls into disarray and the journey is abandoned. They cannot make it without the servant Leo. The narrator, one of the party, after some years of wandering finds Leo and is taken into the Order that had sponsored the journey. There he discovers that Leo, whom he had known first as servant, was in fact the titular head of the Order, its guiding spirit, a great and noble leader" (p. 2).

The concept is one that gained popularity in the 1990s and continued through management trainings and discussions throughout more recent years. The concept had been most frequently applied by individuals in leadership carrying their authority lightly and teaching and gaining compliance through example rather than by diktat. Greenleaf (1977) suggests the following tests determine if servant leadership is working well: "Do those served grow as persons? Do they, while being served, become healthier, wiser, freer, more autonomous, more likely themselves to become servants?" (p. 5)

When creating professional development programs or planning for a staff retreat, these leadership qualities can be effective in obtaining buy-in and building a coalition. Leaders can ask themselves about the intended outcomes for the training or development. Are issues of freedom, health, seeking wisdom, and working more autonomously reasonable outcomes for the training? Does a leader or manager who displays a desire to serve with humility and grace, set an example for employees in the department to behave in the same manner?

CHECKLIST FOR PROFESSIONAL DEVELOPMENT AND TEAM BUILDING SUCCESS

1. **Have a clear and common objective in mind:**
    What do you hope to accomplish with this activity? Solicit feedback from your team about what their priorities are. Remember, "Just having fun" is often just what the doctor ordered. Gain consensus, but recognize you will be hard-pressed to please all the people all the time!

2. **Plan activities that have the capacity to live on:**
    Consider the sustainability of your activities. Can the Professional Development program you bring in, directly impact the work of your staff with students? Does the book club you've organized have the potential for future related activities? "One and done" programs have less potential to "stick."

3. **Spark and leverage the creative energy of the group:**
    Activities that get people using their creative talents help to ensure participants are engaged. As a bonus: creativity leads to flow, and flow is good for our wellbeing.

99

4. **Attend to details:**
   Book rooms well in advance. Send out calendar invitations holding the date and giving participants information about the event so they have something to anticipate. Make flyers and printed materials that engage. Consider using social media as a part of your activity. And, if attending to details isn't your thing...

5. **Identify team members to attend to details on your behalf:**
   By leveraging the strengths of your staff you get the job done and present an opportunity for others to use their strengths in meeting the planning objectives. Bonus: special projects break up the monotony of day-to-day work.

6. **Remember, many hands make light work:**
   Spread out the responsibilities throughout the team. As above, by leveraging the strengths of your staff you get the job done and allow others to use their strengths in meeting the planning objectives.

7. **Don't get stuck in the "we have no budget" trap:**
   Think about the talents of those around you. Invite a faculty member to present on a topic relevant to your team. Watch a documentary on the state of higher education and invite an Administrator from your campus to come foster a discussion afterward. Be creative to get the job done!

8. **Remember that breaking bread together builds community:**
   And, if #7 above is a barrier, make your event a themed potluck, solicit food donations from local restaurants, or plan events during non-meal hours but provide light/healthy snacks or even just coffee. (People will be pleasantly surprised by this gesture).

9. **Take every opportunity to celebrate and acknowledge:**
   Read a kudos email from a student or faculty member about a standout staff person. Offer a public thanks to a team member who recently went above and beyond on a project. Acknowledge the team members who helped organize the event. This time together creates an opportunity to appreciate and celebrate—why not use it?

10. **Invite your team to participate in acknowledging your presenter(s):**
    Write and sign a paper thank-you card, adding short messages from staff. This will go a long way in the goodwill department (particularly if #7 above had you asking for speakers for little or no honorarium) and it will provide your staff an opportunity to reflect on the activity or presentation. Bonus: reflecting with

gratitude on the actions of others helps to increase our capacity for resilience.

DISCUSSION QUESTIONS

1. How do you see generational differences impacting the way leaders and managers approach team building and professional development? How do you see generational differences playing out in terms of employee expectations? Is there a mismatch on your team(s)?

2. Try to identify two or three of the primary barriers to team building and professional development in your department or division. What are some strategies for overcoming them?

3. Is there a way to leverage the generational differences on your team(s) to positively impact the team building and professional development of your staff?

4. As it relates to team building and professional development, what are some challenges that you see for leaders and managers in today's workplace that are different from challenges faced by previous generations? What are some ways to overcome these obstacles?

5. Who are the team building and professional development champions on your team(s)? How can you accomplish delegating these responsibilities in a way that will allow those champions to shine and use their strengths?

Just One Thing

Jacquie Furtado, M.Ed.
Associate Vice President, Strategy Management & Engagement
Ashford University

As a leader it is most advantageous to set yourself up for success. This means bite your work off in manageable chunks, allow yourself to complete what you set out to do and accomplish your goals. All too often, leaders get caught up in the frenetic nature of "everything is important and urgent," forgetting the value of prioritization. By not boiling the ocean (aka--taking on everything) and thinking strategically about your commitments, you cultivate an environment supportive of focus, follow-through and accountability.

This approach further illustrates an importance to take time to reflect, innovate and simply spend quality time with your team. Lead by example and set your team up for success as well. Oh, and don't forget to celebrate the wins!

Part II

Putting It Into Practice

Chapter Seven

Establishing the Supervisory Relationship

KEY TAKE-A-WAYS

- Personal connection and attention are necessary at the very outset of supervision. Good supervision requires rapport and, eventually, a safe trust-based communication between the supervisor and the employee. Failure to create the proper conditions will often result in increased defensiveness and decreased information being shared.
- It is unlikely the employee you are supervising has never been supervised before. This creates the potential for either negative or positive past experiences in supervision. In either event, it is essential for the manager to ask the employee about their past experiences. These past experiences directly inform their perception and expectations of the current supervisory relationship.
- Generational differences, like difference in gender, socioeconomic status, race/ethnicity, ability, religion and politics, can become a hindrance to the supervision process. When bringing up sensitive issues related to personal beliefs or fixed traits such as race/ethnicity, sexual identity and age, the supervisor should do so after establishing some rapport and trust with the employee.

INTRODUCTION

"In the beginning, it is always dark."

The Childlike Empress, *The Neverending Story* (1995)

If you ask a group of higher educational professionals how they feel about the process of being supervised, you typically receive a split reaction. Some view weekly supervisory meetings as a punitive, micro-managing process they dread attending each week. Others view these meetings as an opportunity for growth and learning, and look forward to the opportunity to have an hour each week to reflect, share and organize their work week. It could be that the key differentiator is the time we spend building the foundation and establishing the relationship early on. It is essential for a supervisor to take time to get to know the employee before creating a plan for the person's development or discussing the things they need the employee to do before next week's board meeting.

The chapter is divided into six sections, addressing what we believe are the central concepts needed to navigate the supervisory relationship and develop a connection with the employee. The first addresses the core elements of building rapport with an individual. This is the process of building a connection that lays a framework to develop trust and positive communication. Once rapport and trust are addressed, practical issues such as overcoming negative past experiences from previous supervision, how to address potential defensiveness, the use of humor, and reflections on the concept of an "open-door policy" will be explored. Finally, we engage in a discussion of how to address potential generational differences as they manifest in the supervisory relationship.

1. BUILDING RAPPORT AND TRUST

When sitting down with an employee for their first supervision session, it is important to create the proper conditions and set a proper climate that will increase the likelihood of the supervisee to share personal insight and useful information. Keywords for the approach are friendly, understanding, non-judgmental and supportive. In order to find a deeper level of understanding of the person, the supervisor will have to be sufficiently attentive, and to be able to "see the world through her eyes," (Van der Meer & Diekhuis, 2014, p. 61).

This personal connection and attention are necessary at the very outset of supervision. Good supervision requires an investment in building rapport. For example, communicating with a level of concern and caring provides the building blocks at the beginning of the supervisory relationship. It is upon this foundation that a safe, trust-based communication between the supervisor and the employee has the ability to grow. Developing trust increases the likelihood that the employee will share the information needed to understand the most effective ways to assist them in completing their work. Without trust, the supervisor and employee are locked into opposing sides, each masking and attempting to protect a personal agenda. This is an increased challenge when working with employees who are frustrated, scared, angry, and feeling disenfranchised with the supervision process.

Establishing a good rapport requires finding the sweet spot between too hot and too cold. "Too hot," in this context, is a manager who downplays the need for the supervision to monitor and evaluate the employee's performance. In essence, this is a supervisor who seeks to make a friend rather than focus on the goals of the supervisory relationship. The "too cold" scenario is one in which the serious nature of supervision is emphasized to such an extent that the individual employee responds defensively and fearfully, which leads to a potentially hostile and adversarial process. Finding a balance between hot and cold is an important part of the rapport-building process. Meloy and Mohandie (2014) identified five steps to facilitate this journey (see Table 7.1).

As rapport is developed, trust is increased. This trust is based on a mutual sense of working together to ensure the work performance of the employee stays at an optimum level. Building connection with the employee is easier when there is a focus on the similarities that exist between the supervisor and the employee. This can include simple connections such as hobbies, sports, TV shows, or other interests. The identification of similarities creates a connection between the manager and employee, lowers

Table 7.1 Techniques to Build Rapport

Smiling	This is a universal gesture of goodwill regardless of culture, nationality, or religion. Research indicates that individuals who receive a smile from another feel accepted and not judged.
Listening carefully	Most people do not listen to each other in an open and patient manner. If the interviewer is attentive, is non-judgmental, and shows interest in other people, a very positive emotional dynamic will be established, even if the interviewee is very distrustful and hates what the interviewer represents.
Finding something in common	Identify a characteristic that is shared between the interviewer and interviewee and point that out. It could be marriage, a child, a common geographical area visited, a certain amount of education, or interest in a certain sport. Find it and say it.
Mirroring the interviewee	This refers to mimicking the interviewee's body language and words, which takes attention and practice. If it is done too obviously, it will be noticed and rapport will not result. It may mean sitting the same way, making similar gestures, using some of the same words, even using similar emotional tones of voice.
Avoiding blunders	Allowing the soles of one's shoes to face another person is considered an insult in the Arabic culture. Displaying a cold and unfriendly demeanor is considered an insult. Conveying impatience, such as glancing at one's watch or tapping one's fingers on the table, is considered an insult. Certain gestures may be an insult. Study the culture and know what the blunders are (Nydell, 1996).

defensiveness, lessens objectification, and sets the stage for a sense of mutual goals.

An issue that comes up in supervision is the question of sharing. One lesson we have learned throughout our careers is that what works for one person might not work for others. Some supervisors relish the sharing of who they are and the immediacy of the conflict that this sometimes brings. These supervisors work well addressing difficult issues as they arise and thrive when challenged in thoughtful debate and conversations by an employee. They bring personal examples into the immediacy of the discussion and convey a sense of genuineness and congruence. That being said, sharing of personal information with employees is not for everyone. There is certainly an element of risk, and it raises a question of maintaining boundaries and protecting your personal space. While it is certainly appropriate to choose to limit what you share as a supervisor, just be sure to find something you feel comfortable sharing in order to build a sense of rapport and trust. This could be as simple as having a favorite photograph of a place you like to visit, a sports team object, or having a favorite book on the coffee table. An important element of supervision is transitioning the employee from seeing the supervisor as a cog in the bureaucratic wheels of the organizational process, to seeing them as a person with tasks and goals in front of them to complete.

We generally find ourselves more connected to people when we know something about them. We are more willing to engage with them, lower our defenses, and share information. The power dynamic in supervision has the potential to heighten and intensify depersonalization and objectification in the mind of the employee. Something as simple as a shared love of animals or a sports team or a fun location pictured in artwork all provide an opportunity for the employee to see the supervisor as just another person. An example of self-disclosure is given in the extract that follows.

Reflections on Self-Disclosure and Sharing

My office at Western Kentucky University, where I served as the director of counseling, was like an explosion of objects arranged by someone with attention-deficit disorder. On the walls, you would see a picture of the New Orleans staple Café du Monde, a Mephistopheles marionette from Prague, a Tibetan singing bowl, Bob the ficus plant (yep, he had a name), wooden puzzles, a sand tray, and an hourglass. My bookshelves held figures from the movies Clerks, The Big Lebowski, and The Matrix. Lara Croft hung from one shelf; Finn,

Jake, and Lumpy Space Princess occupied another shelf. Master Chief from the video game series *Halo*, pictures from my white-water rafting trips, a miniature Freud, and a walk-on-water action Jesus filled the other shelf. For me, these objects tell stories about different parts of my life and convey a sense of openness and genuineness to the individuals I saw for assessments, therapy and supervision.

I can imagine about half of those reading right now smiling in recognition at the objects strewn about my office. You appreciate this and have your own collection of puzzles, fidgeting toys for your students, and personal objects around your office. Other readers are engaged in a collective shudder and remember the advice of a supervisor to never put personal objects in the office. Sharing becomes a matter of personal preference. When I share with those I supervise, I have two rules I do my best to follow. First, I ask myself if what I am about to share has a purpose. Is it something I'm sharing to strengthen the relationship? I don't take up ten minutes of the session to tell them about my recent trip to Amsterdam on a whim.

Second, I ask myself is what I am about to share something that I feel comfortable with and if it is an issue I have resolved in my life. I wouldn't share information about a failed relationship if I was still in the process of figuring out my emotions about that relationship. Likewise, I wouldn't share personal information I don't feel comfortable being known around the office. This would include sexual information, inappropriate jokes, or overly personal information.

Brian Van Brunt, Ed.D.
The NCHERM Group

2. OVERCOMING NEGATIVE PAST EXPERIENCES

It is unlikely the employee you are supervising has never been in supervision before. This creates the potential for either negative or positive past experiences in supervision. In either event, it is essential for the manager to ask the employee about their past experiences. These past experiences directly inform their perception and expectations of the current supervisory relationship. There are few more useful questions for a supervisor to ask during the first ten minutes of the first supervision session than "Can you tell me a little bit about your past experience with supervision at previous jobs? I'm wondering, because sometimes employees have had past negative or positive experiences that can give us a starting place when setting our expectations about how this relationship will develop."

For example, a pet-peeve of many employees (authors included) is the distracted supervisor who routinely shows up late for supervision, seems distracted by emails or text messages during the session or who allows for interrupting phone calls and/or knocks on the door when you are meeting. An employee might be willing to share these frustrations if asked directly and these provide insight to the supervisor around several key mistakes to avoid with this (or any) employee.

Some past areas worth exploring during those first few meetings should include:

- What have been the expectations around meeting times, rescheduling, and timeliness of the start time?
- What worked for you when having a difficult conversation? Some people like to have the discussion out face-to-face. Others prefer to get an email or note about the concern and then discuss it a few days later after they have had time to digest the information. What works best for you?
- How did past supervisors communicate with you in a way that was helpful? What are some ways that were less then helpful?
- What are some pet-peeves you have in terms of supervision or when people are monitoring your work?
- What are some things that previous supervisors have said to you that have energized your work? What are some of the things that have had a slowing or negative impact on your performance?
- How have past supervisors talked to you about time off requests and sick days? What worked and didn't work about that process?

While this is not an exhaustive list of questions, we hope this helps give you an idea of how to spend some time during the first supervision meeting exploring potential negative past supervision and management experiences and how to use the answers to these questions to better get out in front of common problems.

3. ADDRESSING DEFENSIVENESS

Addressing defensiveness is essential to establishing rapport and to developing ways to increase the likelihood of the employee to share details and information with the supervisor. Being willing to empathetically listen to the person being assessed helps them begin to trust and be willing to share. One approach to help lower an employee's defensiveness or

110

discourage only one-word answers is the use of open-ended, circular questions.

Robert "Bob" Ross hosted *The Joy of Painting* in the 1980s. It was amazing how he was able to take his paintbrush and create these amazing landscapes of happy trees in such a nonlinear manner. It was almost like watching a magician perform a trick. It was hard to see where the pieces all lined up, but it was obvious that the person had the confidence and plan to move forward to create the painting or perform the trick.

Open-ended, circular questions (rather than questioning directly from a form) can be an effective way of gathering information while allowing employees to share their story. This process tends to help lower the defenses of the employee and conveys a sense of respect as they share a story rather than having the story deconstructed onto a form or into a series of questions that only have meaning for the manager.

Let's face it, many approach their required weekly supervision with an attitude of frustration and annoyance. One goal of the supervisor is to address these emotions in order to obtain some buy-in to the process from the employee. Any resolution involves addressing the individual's frustration and acknowledging the unfortunate nature of the predicament. This doesn't involve agreeing with everything the employee says but instead, empathizing with the frustrating situation they are in. Managers mishandle supervision if they ignore the nonverbal frustration or anger being conveyed by the employee.

One way to lower defensiveness is to listen empathetically. We spend our lives learning to turn our sensitivity dial up, to better detect subtle emotions or nonverbal gestures. Some of us excel at reading what people are thinking based on their facial expressions. This kind of listening creates confidence in people being assessed, that you can handle the information they are willing to share. It may come as a surprise to some, but employees often make decisions about what they will and won't share during supervision based on their comfort level with the manager sitting across from them.

It is helpful to let the employee know when you are concerned or they have shared something that is particularly moving. All of us seek out feedback about our emotions and the information we share with others. People find it refreshing when they get an accurate reflection of what they are thinking or feeling. If the employee says during the interview they have the desire to yell and berate an office colleague, the supervisor does them no good by simply nodding. Some acknowledgement of the disturbing nature of these thoughts is not only helpful, but also expected by the employee. Obviously, an overreaction such as "You can't say such things" will almost guarantee an increase in defensiveness. A more positive reflection (e.g., "That is hard to hear. It sounds like you have some strong feelings about that colleague.") conveys a sense of appropriate reaction.

4. USING HUMOR

Humor, like cooking with a curry spice, is an acquired skill that some people possess and others have not yet mastered. Jokes land well when the timing and quality of the joke matches the audience's expectations. Humor in the workplace works well to lighten difficult conversations and to remind the employee to keep things in perspective. Many supervisors have mastered this skill and use it to defuse difficult situations and convey a sense of light-heartedness and playfulness within the office.

Humor does not work well when it mixes with cruelty or sarcasm. Humor also does not work well when it singles a person out because of their differences and encourages other staff to tease them as part of the workplace culture. Likewise, humor that contains sexist, misogynistic or cultural/ethnic references is always inappropriate when used in the workplace, particularly when used in a relationship where there is a power dynamic between a supervisor and employee. Humor of this type serves only to propagate stereotypes, and is divisive in its impact.

5. OPEN-DOOR POLICY

Many who have worked in higher education have heard about a supervisor's "open door policy." On the face of the statement, we like and appreciate the idea of staff being comfortable approaching a supervisor. The statement is often made to convey to an employee a willingness to always be there for the employee if times get tough or there is a pressing issue they want to talk about. This walk-in policy gives employees a sense that their supervisor is around, willing to listen and open to discussions.

Supervisors should heed two warnings before they announce to their staff that they have an open-door policy in terms of supervision or talking about concerns staff may have. The first is not to offer this kind of policy if there is not a willingness on the part of the supervisor to follow through with it. If a supervisor is prone to get busy with work projects and an employee drops by to discuss a pressing matter, it would be important for that supervisor to welcome the employee in, rather than convey this is not a good time to talk through verbal or non-verbal means.

The second warning around open-door policies is ensuring the supervisor does not use this policy as an excuse to cancel supervisory meetings or other scheduled events. Having a set supervisor time with each staff member in the office is the best way to ensure the manager has an accurate view of how the department operates and the potential for an early heads-up on projects or office conflicts that need to be addressed. Simply leaving your door open as a supervisor and hoping the employees come in when they need to talk is not an effective strategy for managing an office.

Perhaps a better approach is to have some time first thing in the morning or the last thing during the day dedicated to walk-in questions or clarifications from employees. A supervisor could use this time to catch up on non-pressing tasks that would not be difficult to put aside in order to respond to the employees' needs. While this might not sound as welcoming as a policy that allows the staff to stop by anytime during the day, it is a bit more realistic and allows the supervisor to have some time to work on projects without running the risk of seeming upset or out-of-sorts if an employee stops by and interrupts them with a concern.

6. GENERATIONAL ISSUES

Generational differences, like difference in gender, socioeconomic status, race/ethnicity, ability, religion and politics, can become a hindrance to the supervision process. There are certain challenges in bringing up these potential differences that may reduce open and relaxed communication. The employee could take issue with having their personal beliefs, age or traits brought up if presented as a potential problem that needs to be changed.

When bringing up sensitive issues related to personal beliefs or fixed traits such as race/ethnicity, sexual identity and age, the supervisor should do so after establishing some rapport and trust with the employee. It also might be helpful in bringing up the issue from the supervisor's perspective first before asking questions of the employee. For example, "As an older white male and part of the Boomer generation, I may not fully understand how you approach the world as an African-American Millennial. Would it be helpful to talk about some of the potential differences in our experience so we can learn to see things better from each other's perspective?" It should be noted in this scenario, the answer "no" should be respected and other areas should than be explored rather than pushing the issue.

As we have seen throughout the book so far, generational differences have the potential to impact how we each see the world and how we approach important issues such as response to authority, job meaning, future employment goals and trust in the company, college or university. The best approach for a supervisor is to find an opportunity to discuss these differences with their employee with a sense of openness in order to set the stage for future discussion. If the employee is unwilling to discuss the differences, the supervisor should demonstrate respect by being sensitive to generational differences as they present themselves in the workplace.

Table 7.2 Common Missteps to Avoid in Supervision

Ineffective Approach	Effective Approach
"Well, I don't know who you had before in supervision, but I'm here to tell you the way that I do things and how I have found supervision works best in this office."	"Let's talk for a few minutes about some of the ways you have experienced supervision in the past."
"I'm glad you are here. We have a lot to cover today about the upcoming strategic plan we need to submit by Friday. I'm sorry if you had other things you needed to talk about, but we need to do this first."	"I have some time-sensitive projects we need to talk about today in supervision. Can we talk for a few minutes first about your week and then schedule a follow-up time to catch up?"
"I don't really care how supervision went for you before, this is how it is now. You'll have to adjust to this way of doing things."	"Let's talk a bit about that. Perhaps we can find some middle ground in this supervision process where we can both get our needs met."
"We'll have to miss our supervision appointment this week since I have a meeting with the president. Stop by when you get a chance later in the week to catch up."	"Unfortunately, I have to reschedule our supervision time this week. What time works well for you to reschedule?"
"I want you to be able to say anything you want here in supervision. We can talk about work, your family life, love life, and relationships. Anything that might have an impact on your performance."	"I want you to feel comfortable sharing with me any concerns you have, related to work, or your ability to manage any stress you might experience."
"I don't feel like you are very open and honest with me in supervision. It's like pulling teeth trying to get something beyond a yes or no answer from you. Why is that?"	"Let's talk a little about what you feel comfortable sharing with me in supervision and any obstacles or hesitation you might have that has an impact on your trust or willingness to be open."

EXAMPLE FROM THE EXPERT— 7.1: MOVING FROM PEER TO SUPERVISOR

Relationships are predicated on trust. This is never more true than in healthy relationships between a supervisor and his/her staff. With that said, there can be many challenges to establishing trust with new employees. The "us against them" mentality that some bring to the workplace is a common concern; supervisors often find that employees have a notion that individuals in a position of authority cannot be trusted or that they are somehow out to get them. In some cases, more tenured employees bring questions about your skills, qualifications and experience, wondering why they should listen to you, and questioning your approach to problem-solving, or insisting that you don't understand the nuances of the day-to-day work of the office. Still others may bring assumptions of superiority and entitlement.

These common issues that arise when establishing the supervisory relationship may be a result of generational factors having to do with the individual, with the dynamic between supervisor and supervisee and, as is often the case, they most likely arise out of previous supervisory or workplace dynamics that are entirely out of your purview. In any case, these are challenges to overcome that are not for the faint of heart. It is easy to feel downhearted, or to question your place as a leader, when you encounter those who doubt your intentions.

So… How do you establish a strong relationship with those you supervise? Key elements to establishing strong relationships include honesty, transparency, trust, and respect. As the old adage goes, "treat others how you wish to be treated." Most of us want to be treated with respect, wish for the trust of their staff members, and expect honesty and transparency from their team members. This seems like a no-brainer; but sometimes individuals, both new and experienced in leadership roles, go down the slippery slope and engage in behaviors detrimental to their credibility.

In this case, an important factor in leadership is the ability to self-reflect, recognizing when we've compromised our credibility, acknowledge, and set a course to repair the relationship. As I reflect on my first role as manager, I was faced with the particular challenge of moving from peer to supervisor. While you might assume establishing trust and credibility would come easy in this type of situation, this is not always the case. Looking back, I am certain that my promotion to the position of manager was a good decision on the part of my supervisor; however, I remember in the moment having feelings of isolation and frustration. I was ill-equipped to tackle the challenge of transitioning roles. Peers who I had once trusted, confided in, and shared similar professional goals and aspirations appeared to become adversarial overnight. The logical side of my brain could understand the potential reasons for the change in the relational dynamics; but my emotions got the better of me.

On several occasions, I found myself getting caught up in power struggles with staff members with whom I had always connected and shared similar values. Upon reflection, there are a couple of key moments that helped define my approach to establishing strong relationships with my staff, and those experiences have really shaped my approach to relationship management on the move forward. One instance in particular really stands out.

A close colleague, and friend, Hannah, was passionately articulating the details of a situation with her student where she felt we could do more to support the student. I, unfortunately, chose this moment to focus on departmental policy and failed to recognize the nuances of the situation. In hindsight, I am sure my motivation was a desire to establish myself as the "authority" in the discussion. To complicate things further, Hannah, a Millennial, really struggled to accept feedback, and was particularly put off by public forum discussions. As a Gen Xer with a strong sense of empathy, I reflect back on this situation and see that it represented a failure on my part on a number of levels. First and foremost, my primary focus was on my position as the leader—what was good for the student became a secondary concern. Secondly, I failed to acknowledge Hannah's point of view, was dismissive of her and, whether intended or not, demonstrated a lack of respect for the professional expertise she brought to the table. And finally, in what constituted an epic failure on my part, I provided candid feedback regarding the situation in a very public setting.

I left that team meeting feeling terrible, and I knew why. I was dismissive of Hannah, my close colleague and friend, as if her professional opinion, and the skills and expertise that she brought to the table did not matter. How must that have felt for her? This mistake on my part constituted a major learning opportunity. As I indicated above, strong relationships are predicated on trust and mutual respect, and I clearly did not demonstrate either in this particular situation. As a result, I was faced with a decision that would shape my approach to the role of supervisor on the move forward. Rather than listening to Hannah's concerns, her rationale and the resolution that she was recommending, I got hung up on policy and procedure and was very black and white in my response. The real question was: what now? I could take the easy path, sticking to my guns and enforcing the outcomes determined in our team meeting, or I could acknowledge that I made a mistake, and attempt to restore the relationship. I chose the latter, taking three important steps to restore the relationship.

The next day, I requested a one-on-one meeting with Hannah to discuss the situation. I first gave her an opportunity to speak about her experience, and how she felt as a result of the interaction. I then provided her with an account of my experience and how I felt, acknowledging the mistakes that I made in my approach. Critical at this stage was for me to *listen first, share second*. Third and last, we agreed that I would follow her lead, restoring a "student first" focus; we worked together to devise the best outcome for the student.

Approaching staff with trust, respect, honesty, and transparency, strong leaders will continuously reflect on their professional practice, seeking out opportunities for improvement in the way that they conduct their day-to-day interactions with staff. Remember, it is okay to make mistakes in your role as a leader; in fact, it's an absolute certainty that you will. Just be sure that you are taking the time to reflect on your professional practice and are cognizant of the impact and influence that you have on the people around you. Self-reflection and social awareness will go a long way in ensuring you are successful in managing relationships and maintaining credibility and trust—no matter the generations you lead!

Steve Salter, M.Ed.
Director, Student Access and Wellness
Ashford University

DISCUSSION QUESTIONS

1. Consider the key elements you think are essential to review with an employee during the first supervision session. Think of some examples where you have had a boss, director or supervisor apply these elements well during your experience with them. What obstacles did they have to overcome to be able to spend time during the initial meeting to focus on these key elements?

2. Discuss a time where you used humor to lower defensiveness successfully in supervision. Think about a time where you attempted to make a joke or use humor and it ended up creating tension and distance. What are some of the lessons you have learned when it comes to using humor in supervision, management or leadership?

3. Has there been a time where an employee exhibited a high degree of defensiveness with you in supervision? What are some of the challenges in addressing defensiveness when it may be because of generational differences?
4. What has been your experience with an open-door policy? Have you had an experience where this went well and allowed you to bring up an issue with a supervisor when you otherwise would have not brought it up? Have you been disappointed by a supervisor or director who said they had an open-door policy but then did not follow through with that policy?
5. Reflect on some of the common mistakes you have previously made in supervision. How can you work to get out in front of these mistakes in the future?

Just One Thing

Dr. Mitchell A. Levy
Vice President of Student Affairs & Branch Campus Management
Atlantic Cape Community College

*Reflecting on the positive supervisory and mentoring experiences
I have benefited from, I try always to follow the "Golden Rule,"
in other words, treating supervisees as I would like to be treated.
It is important to value the opinion of all employees at all levels
of the organization. I always both strive to admit mistakes
quickly and to give credit to others. I try to develop and reinforce
appropriate boundaries with my staff and I don't ask them to do
something that I am not willing to do myself. I make it clear to
those outside "my area" how I expect my colleagues to be treated.*

*I want staff in my area to know I "have their back." JK Rowling
has used the following quote in her books: "It is the way one treats
his inferiors more than the way he treats his equals which reveals
one's real character." — Rev. Charles Bayard Miliken, Methodist
Episcopal, Chicago. I do not think of staff I supervise as "inferiors,"
but I think the concept applies with respect to how we treat those
both above and below us in the organizational chart.*

119

Chapter Eight

Addressing Common Staff Problems

KEY TAKE-A-WAYS

- When trying to get out ahead of common staff problems, set clear expectations about behavior and consistently monitor difficulties through frequent meetings to address the behavior before it worsens over time. Develop a consistent pattern of supervision with your employees to allow for problems to be identified and addressed early.

- Provide increased monitoring and communication of problem behaviors to allow for early and frequent intervention opportunities. Additionally, seek support and consultation for yourself in order to stay positive and focused when talking with the employee. This may occur through your own supervision or accessing support such as Listservs.

- Problem behavior rarely occurs in a vacuum. Address other staff concerns privately with individual staff members. Discuss generational differences as they relate to the staff reacting to off-mission behavior from an employee.

- When developing a success plan to change an employee's behavior, focus on small, behavioral changes, and meet with them more frequently to monitor their progress. Involve Human Resources and your Employee Assistance Program (EAP) as appropriate.

LOOKING AT HISTORY

Any manager who has been in the field for more than a decade may quickly begin to notice some commonalities in the employees s/he supervises. This chapter consists of ten case scenarios to provide readers with some real-world examples of common yet difficult situations involving staff, and guidance for how best to handle the challenges presented. Each scenario contains a brief narrative, a table of common positive and negative interventions to manage the employee, and a set of discussion questions for further exploration.

While it is important to remember the larger context of the book in terms of approaching generational conflict in the workplace and supervising with a focus on love, care, and hope, this chapter provides some important training tools for those who are tasked with training managers and supervisors.

1. MARK

Mark is a 24-year-old Millennial who has been working in the admissions department for five months. While he demonstrated an impressive level of energy and a passion for the job during his interview, Mark failed to live up to expectations as he completed his training cycle during the first month. He is often late to work and forgets to attend mandatory staff meetings held by the department. When he does attend staff meetings, other staff members see him as "draining all of the energy out of the room." Tour groups often comment on Mark's lack of enthusiasm while he leads tours, and some have commented that he seemed distracted by his phone and fails to answer questions with any degree of interest.

His supervisor, Glenna, is a 40-year-old Generation Xer who has been in her position for the last ten years. She has collected many concerns about Mark from prospective students, parents, and other admissions staff members. Mark shows little initiative when assigned new tasks, often shows up late for meetings with Glenna, and requires constant monitoring to complete assignments and tasks around the office. Glenna is frustrated and not particularly hopeful that Mark will survive his six-month probationary review.

Table 8.1 Positive and Negative Interventions: Mark

Positive Interventions	Negative Interventions
Early identification of problem; conduct focused meetings with Mark to address problem areas	Wait to build up a lengthy list of problem areas to address at the six-month review

Positive Interventions	Negative Interventions
Provide increased monitoring and communication of problem behaviors to allow for early and frequent intervention opportunities	Avoid contact and conflict with Mark because it is difficult, and increases Glenna's frustration
Explore the possible motivations for poor performance	Make assumptions based on Mark's age about possible motivation for performance issues
Set clear expectations about future behavior and consistently monitor how Mark's performance matches those expectations	Adopt a "wait and see" approach until the six-month evaluation and address all of the problems at one time
Address other staff concerns privately with individual admissions staff members	Hold a public staff meeting to address Mark's poor performance

Discussion Questions

1. What are some of the potential reasons explaining why Mark may not be living up to the expectations set forth for his position?
2. How might you approach an employee like Mark if you were his supervisor?
3. What are some ways through which Glenna could address her frustrations with Mark prior to sitting down with him to address his performance issues? Where might she find some support?
4. Glenna can document Mark's poor job performance and then fire him at his six-month review. What are some of the benefits of this approach? What are some of the potential drawbacks?
5. In attempting to change Mark's performance, there is the potential for Glenna to express caring and hope for better future behavior. Discuss the challenge for Glenna if Mark's behavior does not change and Glenna must move forward with separation.

2. ANNA

Anna has always been a bit of a perfectionist. She is a 54-year-old Baby Boomer who has worked in the student activities department for three years. She coordinates events and handles phone calls and tasks for the Vice President of Student Affairs. Anna often works many hours beyond what is required of the job, and always completes her tasks and job duties on time. She is well connected with other departments on campus and serves on numerous committees.

Jess is Anna's supervisor. Jess is a 28-year-old Millennial who recently completed a master's degree in higher education administration. In the past year, Anna has been feeling more and more overcommitted to her job and struggles to take time for herself. She has missed meetings due to committee commitments, and appears increasingly frazzled. Despite her difficulties juggling all her responsibilities, Anna completes her work assignments and continues to outperform other staff members in the department. This creates some stress for others in the student affairs office, who feel they are being compared to Anna in terms of productivity and performance. The VPSA has also noticed that Anna is not in the office as much as he would like due to her over-commitment to projects and committees elsewhere on campus.

Table 8.2 Positive and Negative Interventions: Anna

Positive Interventions	Negative Interventions
Talk to Anna early and often about her workload and stress level	Avoid addressing the issue out of concern that it would just make things worse
Develop a plan of action for Anna to better manage her projects and look at ways to cut back on her committee work	Assume that Anna has the experience and the ability to fix this problem herself
Address staff concerns individually with those that are concerned about their performance compared to Anna's	Ignore staff members' concerns because their apparent jealousy over Anna's strong work ethic isn't really an issue
Monitor Anna's plan of action and update or adapt it depending on how it has been working	Adopt a "one and done" approach and only monitor behavior if there are additional problems
Discuss age differences as they relate to Jess working with Anna	Ignore generational differences and deal with the frustration, since Anna should be able to figure this problem out on her own at her age

Discussion Questions

1. While Anna's job performance remains strong, she seems increasingly stressed and approaching burnout. What are some of the signs you've experienced in terms of stress and burnout?

123

2. Jess may be tempted to ask some personal questions about Anna's home life and her work–life balance. What are the benefits of asking these questions? What are some of the concerns? How can Jess ask, while respecting Anna's privacy?

3. What might be the best way to address the staff concerns over Anna's strong work ethic and how she tends to outshine everyone else in the department? Why is this a concern that needs addressing?

4. Is there a benefit to offering Anna a referral to the school's Employee Assistance Program (EAP)? What should Jess be aware of when making this referral?

5. Discuss the challenges that exist in this case, related to generational diversity.

3. BETH

Beth is a 70-year-old Mature, who, after retiring from a 45-year career as a librarian, wanted to find ways to spend time working with college students. She has worked part-time as an academic tutor for the past seven years and finds her work generally fulfilling, but often needs positive reinforcement from others in the office. When she isn't told that she is doing well, Beth tends to be passive–aggressive, taking longer breaks and making students wait for their appointments. She also becomes mopey if praise from her supervisor isn't immediately provided.

Maria is a 35- year-old Generation Xer who serves as the director of academic advising; she supervises all of the part-time academic tutors, and generally finds Beth exhausting to deal with. Maria is often frustrated by the amount of time she has to spend micro-managing Beth during the day-to-day operations of the department, and has talked to Beth about her lack of initiative, goal planning, and the amount of time she needs in terms of office support and supervision given her part-time position. Beth generally tunes out during these conversations and briefly changes her behavior before falling back into her normal routine.

Table 8.3 Positive and Negative Interventions: Beth

Positive Interventions	Negative Interventions
Hold Beth accountable for her attendance and other tangible behaviors, and develop an action plan for the future	Deal with frustrations with Beth and simply wait until Beth is ready to retire for good
Have a longer conversation with Beth about her need for guidance and praise	Focus on tangible behavior and avoid longer or more detailed exploration of Beth's behaviors
Set clear and measurable goals for attendance and breaks, and hold Beth accountable for her time	Adopt a "live and let live" policy and ignore Beth's concerning behaviors in hopes that they will go away on their own
Reach out to other staff individually to manage their frustrations with Beth	Set up an all-staff meeting and embarrass Beth for her behavior
Have a discussion with Beth about her job goals and what would be reasonable expectations regarding the supervisory relationship	Continue to meet with Beth and praise her to avoid further conflicts and poor behavior

Discussion Questions

1. Beth presents a number of challenges to Maria given her age, her part-time status, and the amount of handholding she needs. How might you address these challenges?
2. There is a temptation to ignore Beth's passive–aggressive behaviors and need for attention in hopes that it will get better or she will eventually leave. What are some of the concerns around adopting this approach?
3. What are some of the generational challenges that exist between Maria and Beth? Are there any assumptions that might create difficulties for Maria if she brought up Beth's age?
4. Discuss the importance of developing a relationship and setting expectations with a staff member like Beth.
5. How do you manage the challenges of supervision when dealing with part-time staff?

4. DAVIS

Davis is a residential life director in his early 20s. He recently moved across the country to take this job and has been in the role for two months. Davis is generally unmotivated in his work and rarely completes the projects he is assigned. During team projects, he does as little as possible and is generally disliked by many of his co-workers in the department. He seems unconnected to the university and has talked openly about wanting to look for a new job at the end of the year.

Kate is Davis' supervisor and is extremely frustrated with his lack of effort, negative impact to the overall department, and recent informal disclosure that he will be looking for a new job at the end of the year. Kate has to prod Davis to complete even the bare minimum requirements of his job, and is often left feeling that it would be better to complete the tasks herself rather than trying to prod him into action. Kate is also in her twenties and is two years into her job as the housing director at the university.

Table 8.4 Positive and Negative Interventions: Davis

Positive Interventions	Negative Interventions
Develop a clear and consistent plan to address job expectations	Address problems as they come up rather than strategically as part of a larger plan
Consider direct conversation about earlier termination if Davis is not content with his current position	Wait until the end of the year when Davis is rumored to leave to terminate him if he doesn't leave on his own
Discuss Davis' behavior directly with him in the larger context of other staff members and office morale	Focus on Davis' behavior and avoid discussing the impact of his job performance on other staff members
Seek support and supervision to keep personal emotions and frustrations with Davis in balance	Become increasingly reactive and angry when talking to Davis due to feelings of frustration with him
Explore the possibility of an HR discussion or EAP referral if Davis' job performance issues do not improve	Fail to address the issue and allow other staff members to talk to Davis directly about their concerns and how his work performance affects them

Discussion Questions

1. What are some ways through which Kate can manage her frustration with Davis' work performance and his attitude within her department?
2. Discuss what approaches you might find helpful in confronting Davis' work performance issues to develop a larger action plan for improvement.
3. At what stage would you involve HR or make an EAP referral with a staff member like Davis?
4. Discuss some of the generational issues that exist between Kate and Davis? What other issues may come into play if other employees react to Davis and his work performance issues?
5. What are the risks of letting Davis continue to behave this way in the hopes that he will simply find a new job at some point?

5. CARLOS

Carlos is a Baby Boomer in his late 40s who has worked for the Information Technology (IT) department for the past ten years. Recently, his work has begun to slip following the worsening of his wife's chronic illness. Carlos is often on his phone during work hours checking in with her or her doctors. He is often late for meetings because of this, and has used up his sick time caring for her. When Carlos is attending meetings, he is often distracted and worried about his wife at home.

Denise is Carlos' supervisor. She is in her early 20s, is single, and is very knowledgeable about IT issues at the university. Denise is often called away from her office to handle network issues and other computer-related challenges. She has tried to be understanding with Carlos, but other employees have begun to complain about having to pick up his missed work. The situation seems to be getting worse, not better.

Table 8.5 Positive and Negative Interventions: Carlos

Positive Interventions	Negative Interventions
Sit down with Carlos and offer him a referral to the campus EAP or counseling support	Begin counseling Carlos and become his singular support to talk about his wife's illness

Positive Interventions	Negative Interventions
Talk with Carlos about what work performance issues can be accommodated given his family situation	Set a clear and firm zero-tolerance restriction on outside phone calls during work hours
Inquire about Carlos' wife and offer him some basic support and a safe place to talk in supervision	Refuse to talk about outside work issues and hold Carlos accountable to his job performance standards
Address staff members' concerns individually while respecting Carlos' privacy	Hold an all-staff meeting to "get everything out in the open" about Carlos' situation and how to solve this problem in the department
Seek additional support and supervision to more effectively develop a performance action plan with Carlos	Denise focuses less on Carlos and his problem and more on the campus' IT needs

Discussion Questions

1. Any time a supervisor begins to explore home life issues with an employee, there can be a potential dual relationship or boundary problem. What are some ways to address this potential challenge with Denise and Carlos?
2. How can Denise offer support while being aware of the potential of becoming a counselor for Carlos?
3. What are some ways to address the office staff's concerns about Carlos' poor work performance? Is there a place for staff members to continue to assist and pick up Carlos' missed workload, or should firmer limits be set?
4. At what point does Denise need to set firmer limits with Carlos regarding his failure to complete his job duties?
5. Would you require Carlos to attend EAP sessions given his difficulty managing his work duties and his wife's illness?

6. VANESSA

Vanessa is in her early 30s and has worked in the registrar's office for a year. Colleagues have expressed concern over her poor attitude towards students and her tendency to lord her power over students making requests for class assignments and schedules. Vanessa looks for conflict in everyday situations and gets into multiple arguments with students and staff each day. Nothing is ever good enough for her, and she seems happiest when telling a student "no" or when arguing with other staff members about an archaic policy.

Kevin is Vanessa's supervisor. He has been at the university for thirty years and is in his late 50s. When Kevin has tried to address Vanessa's attitude and work performance, she has become defensive and aggressive towards him. She turns the tables around by saying things like, "You know, you aren't the best supervisor either. I have my own complaints about how *you* handle *your* job." This deflection makes Kevin defensive and frustrated. He feels at his wits' end in trying to manage her.

Table 8.6 Positive and Negative Interventions: Vanessa

Positive Interventions	Negative Interventions
Spell out Vanessa's work performance problems clearly during supervision and require her to change	Engage Vanessa in multiple back and forth arguments about her work performance
Focus on small, behavioral changes, and meet with Vanessa more frequently to monitor her progress	Tell Vanessa that she needs to change and have a better attitude or she will need to find a new job
Work with HR and the EAP to require Vanessa to alter her behavior	Get into in-depth discussions about why Vanessa acts the way she does and accuse her of being a negative, nasty person
Begin a process of holding Vanessa accountable for her negative behavior during the work day, and call her aside and issue written warnings and suspensions in conjunction with HR	Embarrass Vanessa publicly by yelling for her to pack her things and go home when she is caught being rude to a student
Kevin to seek support and supervision for his own peace of mind when trying to change Vanessa's poor behavior in the office	Talk to other employees in the office to vent about what a problem Vanessa is and how much easier life would be if she would quit

Discussion Questions

1. How have you previously addressed staff behavior like Vanessa's?
2. What are some methods you use to keep your cool in the face of rude, entitled, or outright defensive or aggressive employee behavior? In other words, how do you protect yourself from people like Vanessa, who try to push your buttons when you are correcting their behavior?

3. What might be some underlying issues that are contributing to Vanessa's behavioral problems?
4. At what point does it make sense to involve HR and the EAP in the development of your performance action plan with Vanessa?
5. How do you address the tension between trying to help an employee like Vanessa change her behavior and do her job better, versus documenting her behavior to eventually fire her?

7. FIONA

Fiona is nineteen years of age and works part-time for the bookstore while attending classes to become a nurse. She is often indecisive at work and falls behind other student-workers in the bookstore. During the fall textbook buy-back, Fiona became increasingly confused about what she was supposed to do and rarely completed the work that was assigned to her. Other staff members and student workers call her a "ditz" and wonder how long it will be until she is fired.

Wayne runs the campus bookstore and is in charge of the student-workers. Wayne is in his early 30s and is known by his staff as being very efficient and task-oriented, but overall fair with his employees. Wayne has talked to Fiona several times with little positive change in her behavior. He finds that she has little passion for the work and wonders if she understands half of what he is saying.

Table 8.7 Positive and Negative Interventions: Fiona

Positive Interventions	Negative Interventions
Outline Fiona's job duties in straightforward language and set clear expectations about what needs to change for her to keep her job	Become sarcastic and demand that Fiona "figure this out" or risk being fired at the end of the semester
Attempt to understand where Fiona becomes lost and establish better communication to ensure she doesn't become as lost in the future	Explain the job performance issues quickly to Fiona and tell her to find other staff members to shadow if she still doesn't know what her job is suppose to entail
Share the concerns from the other staff members about her job performance and how her behavior is potentially impacting unit morale	Embarrass Fiona and tell her that no one on the staff likes her and that everyone is talking about her behind her back

Positive Interventions	Negative Interventions
Meet more regularly with Fiona and develop a shadow program with other student-workers to ensure she knows what to do and how to do it	Wait until the end of the semester and don't invite Fiona back to the bookstore, citing that there are enough student-workers without her and she can't remain on the payroll
Talk to Fiona about how she sees the work and question her on some of the stereotypes and myths about the Millennial generation	Lecture Fiona about how she is reinforcing the stereotype about lazy and lost Millennials, and tell her that she is giving their generation a bad name

Discussion Questions

1. What are some of the stereotypes you have heard about the Millennial generation? How would you address these with Fiona?
2. With a large student-worker program at the bookstore, how might Wayne approach the training of his staff to avoid future problems like those he has encountered with Fiona?
3. How might you address staff members' name-calling behind Fiona's back in the bookstore? Is this just simply a natural consequence of her poor performance, or should Wayne take a more active role in dissuading this behavior? How does such behavior impact staff morale?
4. How should a supervisor like Wayne make the decision between spending more time and effort to address Fiona's behavior versus simply terminating her part-time employment and finding someone better suited for the job?
5. How have you addressed the lack of commitment found in some student-workers in part-time positions?

8. SAM

Sam works for the parking and transportation department on campus. She is in her late 20s and has worked for the department for three years. She takes on new tasks with enthusiasm, and is often the first to volunteer to help out in the department. She has strong planning skills but is poor on the follow-through, rarely completing what she has agreed to do.

Chris is Sam's supervisor and genuinely likes working with her. He is also in his late 20s and maintains a strong friendship and supervisory relationship with Sam. He appreciates her willingness to jump up on new projects, but has noticed lately that her follow-through tends to be a problem and a cause for concern among other employees in the department. He is generally hesitant to confront Sam, since he values her friendship and doesn't want to do anything that might jeopardize it.

Table 8.8 Positive and Negative Interventions: Sam

Positive Interventions	Negative Interventions
Engage Sam in a conversation about her lack of follow-through and set expectations for her to change	Avoid confronting Sam due to their friendship and hope the behavior will change on its own
Work more directly with Sam to keep her from taking on more new projects than she can complete, or wait until she has completed those currently on her plate	Avoid giving Sam new assignments and fail to discuss this with her
Develop an office-wide policy to better track projects, that limits all staff members from taking on new projects until they are caught up with current ones	Single out Sam during a staff meeting and embarrass her in front of others about her lack of follow-through
Set up smaller projects for Sam to complete and monitor her projects, giving her clear and direct feedback on her workflow	Set arbitrary deadlines for Sam's projects to be completed and leave her to "sink or swim"
Talk about the challenges confronting Sam about her work habits, given their friendship, but offer clear direction that she needs to be better about completing projects	Become emotional and frustrated at Sam for putting him in the position of having to correct her poor work performance

Discussion Questions

1. What has been your experience with supervisory relationships in which both the supervisor and employee are around the same age? What are some of the benefits of this? What are some of the limitations?

2. Chris has a personal friendship with Sam. How does that complicate his supervision of her? What are some of the problems with having a friendship with your supervisor? What are some of the benefits?

3. What are some ways to address differentials in employee productivity when it comes time to address project speed in a department? Is this better done through individual meetings with those who are falling behind or through a group staff meeting?

4. What are some ways to assist Chris in praising Sam's enthusiasm for new projects while pushing her to work harder to complete her work in a timelier manner?

5. Discuss some strategies to get out in front of differences in employee productivity before a problem becomes more serious.

9. PATRICK

Patrick is 23 years of age and has worked as a trainer for the athletic department for the past three months. He has very close relationships with the students with whom he works, and given his age, is often mistaken for a college student. Rumors that he is dating some of the students on the women's volleyball team have been circulating in the department. Patrick has poorly defined boundaries with the students with whom he works, and has gone out for drinks with them after work.

Lori is 43-years-old and is Patrick's supervisor. She is increasingly concerned that he is too young to be working with college students so close to his age. She has held off having a direct conversation with him about this, and has been gathering reports from other staff members so that she can better confront him about his behavior. But since there have been no direct complaints from students or clear evidence of inappropriate relationships with students, she doesn't feel she can yet talk to him about this. Further complicating the matter is the lack of a clear policy by the university addressing dating between staff and students.

Table 8.9 Positive and Negative Interventions: Patrick

Positive Interventions	Negative Interventions
Discuss the job expectations, boundaries, and workplace behavior expectations between employees and students	Ignore the problem, as there is no clear university policy on staff dating students
Talk about why this behavior is a concern and how it has a potentially negative impact on his ability to perform his job	Embarrass Patrick about his lack of professionalism in front of other staff members during a team meeting

Positive Interventions	Negative Interventions
Address how Patrick can adjust his behaviors through a clear and well-defined corrective action plan	Give Patrick an ultimatum that he either needs to stop his behavior or he will be fired
Review ways through which Patrick can remain engaged with students while maintaining professional boundaries	Feed into the rumors with the other staff members in the department and fail to address the problem with Patrick
Provide Patrick with clear examples of what outside activities with students are permitted and how he can avoid conflict	Lecture Patrick about his age and why he, more than others in the department, must be aware of how people see his activity with young, female students

Discussion Questions

1. Discuss some of the generational issues and how they may hinder or help Lori as she approaches Patrick's behavior.
2. Would Lori have an obligation to intervene if there were no complaints or work performance issues related to Patrick's lax boundaries?
3. How might Lori address Patrick's behavior among the other staff members, given the rumors circulating around the department?
4. What role might Lori play in talking to HR about the lack of clarity about employees dating students at the institution?
5. How have you addressed the issue of workplace romances with staff or faculty members in the past? What are some of the problems with this behavior when it comes to power differentials and Title IX requirements?

10. DAVE

Dave is in his early 30s and has worked for the campus safety department as a dispatcher for the past five years. Dave judicially addresses all the policy violations with which he comes in contact, and views his role as being on the "front lines of a battle" with students at his centrally located dispatch post. As such, he is always on the lookout for a student to report. Students generally don't like Dave, as he always has a lecture ready for them. Additionally, he fosters an adversarial relationship with everyone around him.

Carla, who is in her early 40s, is Dave's supervisor and has been with the university for three years. She is increasingly frustrated with how Dave approaches his job. At first, she found it refreshing that he took policy enforcement so seriously, and appreciated the efficiency with which he completed his job duties. As time progressed, other staff members have shared their frustrations about Dave's militaristic attitude toward enforcement. Dave also has the highest rate of student complaints in the department, and Carla has talked to him on several occasions about adopting a more community-policing approach.

Table 8.10 Positive and Negative Interventions: Dave

Positive Interventions	Negative Interventions
Set clear limits with Dave around his work performance and develop an improvement plan with him to change his behaviors	Demand immediate change from Dave and issue an ultimatum that if he doesn't change he will be fired
Explore the motivation for Dave's approach to the job and discuss how these are in conflict with the department's approach	Engage other staff members in talking to Dave about his behavior and telling him that if it doesn't stop he will be putting his job in jeopardy
Encourage Dave to direct his energy for the job towards other tasks and limit some of his student interaction	Tell Dave that he is no good with people and place him a position where he no longer has any student contact
Offer staff-wide training on community-policing concepts and help all staff members understand the department's mission	Address Dave's behavior publicly with other staff members to embarrass him into compliance
Have another employee provide some role modeling for Dave in terms of what behaviors are expected of him on the job	Ignore the problem and be grateful that Dave is at least doing some parts of his job well

Discussion Questions

1. What steps could Carla take with the entire department to ensure that all employees understand the departmental philosophy and adopt it in their roles?
2. If Dave is unwilling to change his behavior, how might Carla develop an action or success plan to progressively improve Dave's behavior?

3. How would you handle the staff backlash to Dave's behavior in a productive and solution-focused manner?

4. Given that Carla has addressed this behavior previously, at what point should she shift to involving HR and moving towards a separation, versus continuing to try to improve his work performance?

5. What are some of the generational challenges that may exist with Carla addressing Dave's behavior? How might gender play a role in addressing Dave's work performance issues?

FINAL THOUGHTS ON ADDRESSING COMMON STAFF PROBLEMS

Stories bring us together. One of the reasons we used this type of teaching method in this chapter was to highlight the commonly encountered staff problems in a manner that allows staff to put themselves into the perspective of the supervisor trying to bring about change. While a departure from the style of the rest of the book, the authors felt this was a useful way to help the reader wrestle with the practical challenges of putting the concepts outlined in the previous chapters into practice.

Additionally, this approach allows for this chapter to become a standalone training tool for supervisor training discussions and workshops. Readers are encouraged to share these stories in a group setting, and work through the discussion questions to better grow and learn together.

Just One Thing

David J. Denino, LPC, NCC
Director Emeritus, Counseling Services
Adjunct Professor, Clinical Mental Health Program
Southern Connecticut State University

*Good leadership and supervision are bestowed in many ways.
For leadership and supervision it's my simple recipe of: one part
"how would I like to be treated," and one part "is the fairness
factor applied to each person I touch." Being true to these two
personifications will bring about the qualities of what kind of
relationship you will have with colleagues, students, and others in
your life. Oh, and its foundation is based in a quote from Patch
Adams, "The most radical act anyone could ever commit is to
be happy," together with Randy Pausch's quote, "Never, ever
underestimate the importance of having fun."
Bam! Now you can lead.*

Chapter Nine

Avoiding Common Supervisor Mistakes

KEY TAKE-A-WAYS

- Changing well-established behavioral patterns is almost always an uphill battle involving two steps forward and one step backwards. Any plan to adjust work performance and supervisory relationships should be clearly defined and measurable to allow for monitoring and future adjustments. Jumping immediately to the action stage will likely bring about resistance and defensiveness from staff. First, try to understand the resistance to change through an open conversation, and attempt to find a common ground of agreement.

- Gossiping and treating staff inconsistently can create a hostile and difficult atmosphere for everyone in the office. This can come from a lack of training and commitment to the supervision process. One way to avoid these problems is training supervisors in management and leadership when they are initially hired.

- While having a close relationship with employees can help in fostering a positive office environment, it is important to set boundaries, and, as a supervisor, not use your employees as a group of captive friends. Good supervisors find a middle ground between friendliness and professionalism.

- Dating within the office has the potential to create problems in a number of areas. Relationships with power differentials in an organization create the perception of bias and special treatment. If a relationship is to happen, it is a best practice to reassign the supervisory responsibility to a different supervisor. It is also better to work directly with Human Resources to discuss the relationship, and to brainstorm ideas to keep the relationship from being exploitative or creating the perception of special treatment.

SOME MORE STORIES

One of the more difficult tasks involved in supervision and leadership in higher education is turning the mirror around to the supervisor's approach and behavior, realizing that sometimes the problem isn't the employee. Unless we're willing to do that, we may not be able to see that sometimes it's the supervisor who is causing a conflict or making a problem worse. In this chapter, we will review nine common missteps supervisors make, and offer some practical suggestions to bring about change in a supervisor who is engaging in ineffective practices. Each of the case scenarios that follow highlights one such misstep, and then offers a set of discussion questions and reflective exercises to bring about a positive change in behavior.

In addressing supervisors' behavior, it is important to remember that all supervisors have had moments in which they weren't at their best or able to bring their "A" game with a particular employee. As such, this chapter isn't intended to shame managers' bad behavior, but instead offer a path to improving their interactions with the employees they supervise.

1. KAYE

Kaye loves all of the employees she supervises like they are her children. Kaye is 52-years-old, has worked as a dean of students for the past 20 years, and tends to form overly close relationships with all of her employees, asking about their personal lives and staying connected with each of them on Facebook and other social media. While this works well for many of her employees, some wish Kaye wasn't so involved in their personal lives, and posted so often on their Facebook pages.

Kaye has had some difficulty confronting employees on job performance issues, as she often feels that doing so will put the friendships she has formed at risk. She often has parties at her house and invites all of the staff members to come over, and pesters those who don't feel comfortable attending them. In addition, she often goes out for drinks with her employees after work and shares detailed stories about her romantic relationships with them, as well as the ups and downs of her personal life.

Discussion Questions

1. What are some of the problems with Kaye's approach to boundaries at work? Have you had a supervisor like Kaye before? What were some of the difficulties that occurred in your relationship?
2. While there are many good things about Kaye's ability to connect with her employees and develop a close-knit department, there are also problems that occur in terms of boundaries and privacy. Describe some potential difficulties.
3. What are some ways in which Kaye can pull back a bit without creating tension among employees who have become accustomed to her overly casual interaction style?

Reflective Exercises

1. Make a list of the pros and cons of having flexible boundaries and more personal relationships with those whom you supervise.
2. Come up with an example of when having a more personal relationship with an employee has been beneficial in the supervisory relationship in terms of setting expectations and holding the employee accountable for work performance.
3. Discuss a time when having an overly close relationship with an employee made it more difficult for you to carry out your supervisory responsibilities.

Bringing It All Together

Kaye may mean well in her relationship with her employees; however, the level of personal connection and mixing of work and home life has the potential to make some employees uncomfortable. It may be difficult at times to switch from an easygoing friendship to having to set limits with her supervisees. While this might be a transition that Kaye can handle, some of her supervisees may react poorly to Kaye setting firmer limits on their work performance. Likewise, some employees may feel pressed to maintain a personal, out-of-work relationship with Kaye by attending her parties and drinking together after work to be seen as "good employees."

While having a close relationship with employees can help in fostering a positive office environment, it is important to set boundaries, and, as a supervisor, not use your employees as a group of captive friends.

2. CARTER

Carter is in his early 30s and works in student accessibility and success services. He has been a supervisor in the department for three years, and has been having a relationship with a subordinate staff member named Jeff. They hit it off quickly in the office and during their one-on-one meetings. Jeff initiated the relationship with Carter. They both decided it would be better to keep their dating quiet from the rest of the office at first to avoid unnecessary drama or the appearance of favoritism in the eyes of the other staff members, but after they had been dating for several months, Jeff began to drop hints to some of his co-workers about his relationship with Carter. This quickly spread throughout the office, and now everyone knows they are dating, but it isn't brought up publicly.

Most of the staff are happy for Jeff and Carter, and both are generally liked. Some employees joke about Jeff getting special treatment from Carter, but most of those comments are said in a joking manner with little tie to reality. Both are happy in the relationship, and while Jeff has an idea that many people in the office know that they are dating, Carter remains in the dark about the fact that others know about the relationship.

Discussion Questions

1. What does your HR policy say about supervisors dating employees? Are there some conditions where this behavior is allowed? What are some of the potential Title IX implications of the relationship in the workplace?
2. What are some of the potential difficulties that could come from the relationship in the future?
3. Would the relationship be less of an issue if both Jeff and Carter were equally situated colleagues and Carter wasn't in a power differential role with Jeff? What is your school's policy on staff and faculty dating when they have equal power roles?

Reflective Exercises

1. While everything seems to be going well so far, think about some potential "hotspots" that could arise in the future if the relationship ended, or if other employees complained about favoritism. Consider

some of the difficulties that could occur if Jeff ended the relationship. What are some potential challenges if Carter ended the relationship?

2. What are some of the ways in which the relationship could continue without potential conflict with staff or the exploitation of the power differential between Jeff and Carter? Think about how that might change if Jeff and Carter were just having casual sex versus being in a committed relationship.

3. Consider the issue of the secrecy in the relationship. What are some of the added problems that occur when the relationship occurs initially away from others in the office? What might be some of the implications for students receiving services from the office if the relationship becomes more widely known around campus?

Bringing It All Together

Dating within the office has the potential to create problems in a number of areas. While Jeff and Carter may have had the right intention at the start by keeping the relationship private, it is hard to keep anything private in a small campus department. Relationships with power differentials in an organization create the perception of bias and special treatment. If a relationship is to happen, it is a best practice to reassign the supervisory responsibility to a different supervisor. It would be wise to work directly with Human Resources, obtaining their input and views on the relationship, and brainstorm ideas so as to avoid an exploitative relationship and/or any perception of special treatment.

3. FRANK

Frank, who is in his early 50s, works in the registrar's office. He has been at the university for 20 years, has a deep knowledge of its policies and procedures and frequently launches into lengthy diatribes about the rules to any student who happens to cross his path. He is known for lecturing others, and has very little sympathy or understanding for those who ask him questions. He tends to treat others with disdain and a certain level of annoyance when it comes to addressing issues around transcripts, parental notification, and access to records.

Those under Frank's supervision are treated in the same way as students. He sees every problem as having a clear policy and procedure solution, and has very little patience for those who do not know the rules as well as he does. He is clear with employees that he is not interested in talking about anything beyond what is required for work, and avoids any attempt to discuss social issues or anything related to home life.

Discussion Questions

1. What are some of the challenges involved in attempting to change the behavior of an entrenched, long-time employee who seems unwilling to adopt new approaches to working with people?
2. What are some of the additional qualities that would be helpful for Frank to develop in order to be more effective in carrying out his workplace responsibilities?
3. How might Frank's attitude impact others in the department and around campus?

Reflective Exercises

1. There is often a temptation to "not fix what's not broken" when working with long-term employees who may have attitudes or approaches that no longer work well. Getting such individuals to change may not seem worth the frustrations it will cause. What is your institution's mission in regards to helpfulness and good customer service, and how does Frank's behavior contrast to the approach the university attempts to set forth?
2. Given Frank's appreciation for the rules and policy/procedure, what might be the most effective approach when trying to change his behavior? How might Frank adjust when approached by a senior administrator with clear behavioral expectations?
3. One challenge in addressing this type of behavior is setting up a corrective action plan that reaches beyond a "one and done" approach. The most successful plans will likely involve monitoring Frank's behavior with subsequent adjustments, to better measure how he adapts to change. How might you develop such a plan with an employee like Frank?

Bringing It All Together

Changing well-established behavioral patterns is almost always an uphill battle involving two steps forward and one step backwards. Frank has been in his position for a long time, and taking some first steps to address his resistance to change will likely help the process move forward much more cleanly. Any plan to adjust Frank's work performance and supervisory relationships should be clearly defined and measurable to allow for monitoring and future adjustments. Jumping immediately to the action stage will likely bring about resistance and defensiveness from Frank. First, try to understand his resistance to change through an open conversation, and attempt to find a common ground of agreement.

4. ERICA

Erica is in her early 30s and has been employed as the university's food services director for the past two years. Her staff universally does not care for Erica's style of micro-managing leadership. She has very high expectations, and has made it clear that she is not interested in others' opinions of how they approach their work. She meets frequently with all of her supervisees, and gives them very little room to work on their own.

Erica approaches her job with a high level of seriousness and determination. She has exceptionally high standards, and believes that any wavering from those standards will result in a decrease in the overall quality of the university's food services. Erica often says, "I am getting paid to monitor and watch employees to ensure they are doing what they are being paid to do. If anyone has a problem with that, they can take it up with my boss." Erica doesn't trust her employees, and often sees them as working against her desire to provide exceptional quality service to the university.

Discussion Questions

1. What are some of the central flaws in Erica's approach to running her department?
2. Erica fosters an environment of mistrust and frustration. What are some of the ways in which frustrations will come out in the employees she supervises?
3. What are some ways to start a conversation with Erica about adjusting her approach to running her department? What are the obstacles to be aware of when talking with her?

Reflective Exercises

1. Erica is over-focused on the rules, to the detriment of building a community of trust and shared goals with her employees. What are some ways to begin a discussion with her about the need to lower her defensiveness and find a common area to push forward?

2. Erica likely has created an office environment where employees have difficulty thinking for themselves or trusting that Erica would be in their corner if they needed something from her. This kind of environment fosters a dependence on Erica and typically creates a perpetual cycle that is difficult for her to break. What are some first steps that would help "set the stage" for Erica to change some of her behavior and begin to build trust with her employees?

3. As an institution, what are some ways to get out in front of this type of supervisory problem? While we obviously want supervisors who are willing to monitor their employees' work performance, most can appreciate the undesirability of having their work micro-managed by another person. What type of training or support does your university offer for those who are new to the supervision process?

Bringing It All Together

Erica faces a common dilemma for new supervisors. She has internalized the importance of monitoring employee compliance to ensure the fulfillment of their job duties—which is a positive thing—but the way she carries out her monitoring duties means that even when staff members perform well, they likely feel unappreciated in their work and constantly on the verge of being in trouble with Erica. While Erica's philosophy may have been noble at the start, it's important for her to build a more positive workplace community of trust and individual responsibility with those she supervises.

5. DEVON

Devon is 47-years-old, supervises several staff in health services, and has worked at the university for the past five years. He sets forth unclear expectations for those under his supervision, and most of his staff feel confused about what is required of them. He is inconsistent in his own work, and alternates between micro-managing his staff and ignoring all of them for weeks at a time. Most think that Devon is a bad supervisor, but don't tell him this directly.

When Devon becomes frustrated, which is often, he shares too much about his feelings towards other staff members in the department. He gossips freely with some employees and shares personal- and work performance-related information with staff members. An example of this occurred during one supervision meeting with Darcy, when he said, "Darcy, you didn't do well on this annual performance evaluation—that is true. But compared to Mark? You look like the ideal employee. Keep it in perspective."

Discussion Questions

1. What might be some motivations behind the way Devon acts towards those in his department?
2. What are some steps you would take to change Devon's behavior through an action plan? What are some of the potential obstacles to this action plan being carried out?
3. When supervisors behave inconstantly, it sends the message that such behavior is allowable for those under their watch. How might you engage Devon in a conversation about how his behavior is impacting the department, without eliciting a defense reaction from him?

Reflective Exercises

1. Rumors and gossip can have a cumulative negative impact on an entire department. Discuss some ways in which Devon's gossiping with his supervisees makes it difficult to foster an atmosphere of trust and a sense of community among the staff.
2. Devon has been engaged in this behavior for several years. How might his supervisor address the behavior in a way that could bring about change, given the entrenched nature of Devon's attitude and the negative effects his inconsistency has already had on the department? At what point should Devon be considered for termination, transfer, or demotion?
3. What are some of the potential HR and employment actions to which Devon's gossiping and rumors expose the department when providing students with health care? If a student overhears Devon sharing information or sees the inconsistency in the department, how might this inform that student's attitude about the clinical care being provided?

Bringing It All Together

Devon has created a hostile and difficult atmosphere for everyone he supervises through his gossiping and inconsistency. The department may already be seen by students as being ineffective, and compromising the privacy of student health information. Devon's supervisory approach should be addressed quickly and monitored over time to track how he is complying with new standards for his conduct. His lack of training and commitment to the supervision process should provide an example of the importance of training supervisors in management and leadership when they are initially hired.

6. TARA

Tara is the 62-year-old head of the biology department. She has been at the college for ten years. Tara intimidates other professors in the department with threats and ultimatums issued to get them to perform tasks assigned to them or to leave her alone when she does not wish to be bothered. Department employees generally avoid interacting with Tara because she has a history of starting arguments and causing untold problems for professors.

The department-head position is a rotating one, and many faculty members in the department are just counting the days until Tara's "reign of terror" ends in another year and a half. One faculty member made the mistake of challenging Tara on a departmental budget request, and that professor now has all of his budget requests micro-managed, with very few purchases getting approved.

Discussion Questions

1. What avenues are available for the department staff to attempt to address Tara's behavior as the chair? What are some of the obstacles that may keep faculty members from bringing their concerns forward?
2. What process does your university have in place to vet and/or train new supervisors prior to assigning them employees to oversee? In a perfect world where money and time were not hurdles, how might you set up a training program for staff or faculty members moving into management or leadership positions?
3. What may be some of the motivations behind Tara's supervisory style? How might you use this information to develop a plan to change her approach?

Reflective Exercises

1. There is a temptation when dealing with an employee like Tara to avoid discussing the problem, instead waiting out the conflict until there is a position change. Discuss the concerns that others in the department may have about confronting Tara. How might they find a way around such concerns?

2. There appears to be a case of retaliation against an employee who challenged Tara. Retaliation can be difficult to prove in cases like this, where all budget requests are typically scrutinized and subject to rather contextual approval. What might be some ways to prove retaliation?

3. How might HR become involved in this situation with Tara? In your opinion, what are the pros and cons of attempting to train Tara to improve her supervisory abilities, versus looking at a termination of the position or reduction in her supervision duties?

Bringing It All Together

Tara moved from a standard faculty position to a supervisory one within the department. In adapting to the new position, she began to bully and threaten other professors in the department. It is likely that Tara is not cut out to be in a leadership or management role, and Human Resources may have to become involved in making a change in departmental leadership. This case raises the importance of training and vetting new supervisors, offering both education and support for their new job responsibilities.

7. JACOB

Jacob is 25 years of age, has worked for residential life as a hall director for the past two years, and has fifteen resident advisors on his staff, approaching each of them as a personal friend. He often shares details of his personal life and his relationships with the RAs, and expects them to do the same. While he doesn't describe it this way to the director of residential life, Jacob views his staff as an extended family. As such, his supervision sessions with them are opportunities to share and catch up with extended family members.

Jacob is well liked by his staff and has infrequent problems getting his RAs to perform and comply with the requirements of the job. Most of his staff members leave their positions each year, so he always has new RAs to supervise. Jacob approaches any staff challenges (e.g., RAs not creating their bulletin boards, attending meetings, or confronting residents) with a plea to the RAs as personal friends, and statements about his disappointment with their behavior. This typically works well to get the RAs back on track.

Discussion Questions

1. Given that there aren't many complaints about Jacob's supervisory techniques, how would you approach a conversation about how he gets compliance out of his staff?
2. Discuss a potential conflict that could occur given Jacob's approach to supervision. How might this conflict be addressed before it grows into a larger issue?
3. Describe how you approach boundaries with employees you supervise. Where do you draw the line on sharing personal information? What are some of the implications of requiring supervisees to talk about personal issues during work?

Reflective Exercises

1. Is there a problem with the way Jacob approaches his job as long as all the RAs are completing their work and there aren't complaints from students? Discuss past supervisors you have had like Jacob, and list what the positives and negatives are when a supervisor develops this kind of relationship with supervisees.
2. Think about other resident directors in the department. What kind of impact might Jacob's approach to supervision have on other RDs who take a more traditional approach to supervision?
3. Why is maintaining boundaries with those whom you supervise important? What are some signs that a supervisor's boundaries with those under their supervision are too lax? On the other side of the spectrum, what are some examples of boundaries that are too limiting and strict?

Bringing It All Together

While Jacob means well and has some success supervising those RAs assigned to him, his approach to supervisory boundaries is fraught with problems. There haven't been many complaints as of yet, but when complaints do come in, they are likely to have a larger impact on the university. While the supervisor does not want to be distant from his employees, being overly friendly and sharing too much personal information makes it difficult to step back and hold the employees accountable for their work performance. In this situation, Jacob is working with younger, more impressionable employees. Setting clear expectations and remaining focused on ensuring the RAs fulfill their job requirements is easier to accomplish within the bounds of a professional relationship.

8. MARIS

Maris works in academic affairs and oversees a department of eight doctoral students serving as teaching assistants. Maris is 32 years of age, has been at the university for six months, is quiet and introverted by nature, and finds it difficult to carry on conversations with others in the department. While those around her often see her as nice and kind, few know much about Maris and wonder about her personal life.

Maris becomes very sensitive when faced with those kinds of questions, and often feels that others are talking about her behind her back. She is also very sensitive to any kind of criticism from the graduate students or the department head, and often excuses herself from her desk to collect her thoughts in the bathroom. Maris avoids confronting the graduate students when their work performance drops, in hopes that they will leave her alone as well.

Discussion Questions

1. How might you address Maris' supervision of her graduate students if you were her department head? What would most likely be helpful for Maris to improve upon her supervision skills?
2. Is being quiet or withdrawn always a mark against a supervisor? How can someone who is more introverted excel in management and leadership?
3. How do generational issues play out with Maris in this case, assuming the doctoral students are all between 24 and 26 years of age?

Reflective Exercises

1. What are some traits that might make someone particularly well suited to be a supervisor? Are there some personality traits that would preclude someone from leadership and management positions? Are the needed attributes teachable, or is it a case of "you either have it or you don't?"

2. How do you handle criticism from subordinates or a supervisor? What are some ways that criticisms can be delivered to increase the likelihood of their being received well? What are some ways that criticisms are shared that can increase a person's defensiveness?

3. Discuss some first steps Maris could take to be more open to critical feedback from her supervisor. Would this feedback be easier to hear directly through a conversation, over email, or in another (e.g., letter) format? What is your preferred method for receiving feedback from others?

Bringing It All Together

Maris has some personality traits that make it difficult for her to supervise graduate students as part of her new position. This likely could present an opportunity for Maris to lean on her supervisor for support and to potentially grow and develop enhanced skills for working in a supervisory role. However, that may be a difficult task, given Maris' sensitivity to critical feedback. Care should be taken to assist Maris and inspire hope that this is a skill set she can develop. There may also be room for a discussion about whether Maris is well-suited for supervisory work, which could help her make the choice to retool her career to find work that's a better fit for her.

9. GARY

Gary is 57-years-old, has worked for the university's police department as a sergeant for the past 14 years, and is known as a straight shooter by those he supervises, taking little guff from those who don't agree with his points of view. He typically deals with others' conflicting views or opinions through aggressive and loud behavior, often becoming red-faced and angry, and shouting down any opposition at staff meetings and during individual supervision meetings.

Gary believes there is little room for disagreement on the police force, and has been known to adopt an "it's my way or the highway" approach to leadership. When officers have dared to question his authority or methods, he has sent them storming out of his office with a wave of curses and insults. Employees in the department tend to give Gary a wide berth and assume that his attitude is a leftover vestige from his military service.

Discussion Questions

1. What are some ways to address Gary's approach to supervision and management? Who might be best to approach Gary about his behavior?
2. What are some of the problems with Gary's intimidation and yelling? What concerns might students have about this type of behavior from the police?
3. What are some possible reasons for why Gary may approach his management and leadership role this way? Is this something that is likely to change with correction, or something that is likely set in stone? What are some ways a supervisor could address Gary's problematic behavior to lower his defensiveness and increase the likelihood of a positive outcome?

Reflective Exercises

1. Are there certain departments on campus that are known for particular styles of leadership and management? What are some examples of different departments' approaches to supervision and management? Do the departments draw employees with a predisposition for this kind of behavior, or do the departments themselves contribute to the creation of the behavior?
2. At what point should an institution involve HR to address a problem like Gary's behavior on campus? How might an HR department address Gary? Should other staff members be involved in such a scenario? What would be an example of a good corrective action plan for an employee like Gary?
3. What are some of the potential generational issues in this case? Discuss how each generation (i.e., Mature, Baby Boomer, Generation Xer and Millennial) might approach supervision, management, and

leadership. Are certain generations more likely to be willing to adapt? Are some less likely to change?

Bringing It All Together

Gary comes from a military background and a generation where gruff and direct behavior (particularly among law enforcement) may have been the norm. Confronting Gary directly to successfully engage him in a process to bring about change would likely be challenging. Yet, his yelling and intimidation in the workplace is unacceptable—particularly in a higher education setting and within a department where level-headed coolness should be encouraged. The other problem is that his behavior makes it difficult for the officers under his supervision to share information and communicate with him. Gary's behavior further reinforces the stereotype that cops don't need help, training, or anything else to do their job well.

FINAL THOUGHTS ON AVOIDING COMMON SUPERVISOR APPROACHES

It is never easy to gaze into the mirror of self-reflection and see parts of ourselves that may not be the most flattering, or those traits that do not put us in the best light. The use of narrative and stories is one teaching method to help readers better explore these concepts in a more practical, application-based manner. We all have stories that we can tell about our greatest failures and times where our supervisory or management skills fell well short of the mark.

The stories above are provided to give the reader an opportunity to apply the theoretical concepts mentioned earlier in the book in practice. Reflective exercises can be used to help augment a supervisory journal or more informally, to encourage leaders to spend some time considering these essential concepts.

Just One Thing

Amber Eckert
Vice President, Student Services
Alliant International University

Often times, the role of a leader is to deliver information and carry out actions that are "not pleasant." This may be providing performance feedback that is not in line with the employee's self-perception of their actions; informing the team that due to recent budget cuts, a trip to a professional conference has been cut; or having to demote an employee due to organizational restructuring.

The ultimate challenge in these types of "not pleasant" scenarios is to maintain a balance of feeling and expressing empathy for the impact the information has on the individual (or team), but also recognizing that the team will take much of their cue for how to react from yours. I'm not recommending "putting on a happy face," but it is important to realize that your team is counting on you to help them find a path to acceptance and resolution, and modeling moving forward is a key part of that process.

When delivering "not pleasant" information, be authentic in your interactions with individuals, but also cognizant of your responsibility to model moving forward.

Chapter Ten

Three Unexpected Leadership Challenges
Not For the Faint of Heart

KEY TAKE-A-WAYS

- While having an understanding of the potential generational diversity within a system undergoing organizational change can be helpful, having a leader with a steady hand and calm head through the rough waters of change is essential.
- The key to success lies in more fully understanding the motivations of the other person, system or politics before selecting the most effective approach to managing the situation.
- When personal tragedy strikes, supervisors become a critical source of support to both individuals and their teams. Possessing an understanding of the core concepts related to grief and loss help position us to be effective when navigating through such issues with our staff.

Some leadership challenges are inherently more complex than others. In this chapter, we will explore three distinct challenges of leadership: *Organizational Change, Surviving a Difficult Boss or Colleague*, and *Grief and Loss in the Workplace*. We have invited our Examples from the Experts authors to write their very personal stories of traversing these challenges, and layer them against the generational dynamics at work in these situations.

1. ORGANIZATIONAL CHANGE

While it may be true that *"The only thing constant is change,"* it sits in stark contrast to the slow melting pace of the glacier that is higher education. It is possible, then, that when organizational changes occur within a higher education setting, they are even more upending to a system not well known for its agility. Certainly, headlines confirm that higher education *is changing*, and colleges and universities are succumbing to the effects of these changing conditions. Downsizing, restructuring, campus mergers and, as we've seen across the United States, campus closures, are just some of the harbingers of organizational changes across higher education.

While there is no shortage of systems-level research on the topic of higher education and organizational change, this is not the focus of our discussion (Arum & Roksa, 2011; Bok, 2013). Rather, we invite our readers to consider their experiences, and to examine the practical realities of leading teams through change. In their work, *Reframing Organizations*, Bolman and Deal (2013) observe organizational change through a four frame model that includes the "human resource, structural, political and symbolic frames." This work explores potential barriers to change and the essential strategies required in order to effect change successfully.

These barriers include the "individual feelings of loss of control, a disruption of the current patterns of roles and relationships, conflicts between winners and losers, and loss of meaning for the recipients of change" (p. 392). Table 10.1 combines Bolman and Deal's four frames with the potential for change agency across generations.

Leaders can leverage their knowledge of generational characteristics when considering change processes. Matures often bring wisdom and stability to teams experiencing change. Their sense of loyalty and hard work, and their senior positions within organizations make them key players in change processes. Inviting the Millennial and Boomer with their

Table 10.1 Agents of Change across Generations

Frame	Human Resource	Structural	Political	Symbolic
Need	Learning	Realignment	Negotiation	Grieving
Issue	Loss of control	Disruption of current patterns of roles and relationships	Conflicts between winners and losers	Loss of meaning
Millennial	✓	✓		
Gen X				✓
Boomer		✓	✓	
Mature	✓	✓	✓	✓

Adapted from Bolman, L.G. & Deal, T. E., *Reframing Organizations* (2013)

optimistic tendencies to lead teams in the process of moving forward helps to ensure that team members feel a sense of control, and frees them from becoming "anchored" to the past. Millennials often possess the flexibility to be less invested in the current patterns of roles and relationships and can be leveraged to reduce uncertainty by leading the learning and development process that is fundamental to successful change.

Boomers, through their formal and informal senior roles within teams, as well as their sense of optimism and teamwork, can be ideal candidates to negotiate the conflicts between the "winners and losers" in the change process: those who benefit from the new direction and those who do not. Gen Xer's, often known for their high empathy, can position themselves to be leaders in the grieving process, often assisting colleagues through change and helping them to find meaning in the process.

In our first Example from the Expert, Dr. Amy Murphy encourages leaders to think about organizational change and restructuring as an opportunity to better serve students. By taking this approach, leaders can help staff to move through the change process in a way that honors their experience, while simultaneously helping them to orient in alignment of the organizational transition ahead of them.

EXAMPLE FROM THE EXPERT—
10.1: NAVIGATING THROUGH ORGANIZATIONAL CHANGE

Times of organizational restructuring are difficult and scary. Employees can feel surrounded by uncertainty and unanswered questions. The detailed scrutiny that often comes with organizational restructuring creates a fear of how our roles and responsibilities will be valued in the changing environment. Having experienced a number of significant organizational changes, sometimes within a brief period of time from the last, I understand how these critical moments have the potential to positively or negatively influence the organizational climate and the individual employees.

A leader must first recognize when a significant change is occurring. I have experienced restructuring processes that involved external consultants leading a series of meetings with the staff to inform and plan for the change; reorganizations announced via press release and group staff meetings with significant role and responsibility changes; and slight priority shifts that result in minor differences for the workplace. The first and second cannot be missed, but the last can occur quickly without the impact on the staff being noticed.

Regardless of the type of organizational shift, I believe that during times of change the successful leader exhibits traits that are reassuring to the staff, honest about the situation and available information, and presents an authentic response. I can think of experiences when employees lost jobs during restructuring. As a leader in the organization, it is okay to show sadness or uncertainty during that difficult time. Being communicative and truthful about what information is available regarding the decision and giving employees an opportunity to grieve the loss of their colleagues and friends is essential. It's also important to begin to refocus on the mission of the organization and how the organizational shift impacts the ability to achieve organizational goals.

Sometimes a restructured organization can result in new job responsibilities for staff. Leaders who are able to evaluate an employee's strengths and weaknesses and listen carefully to how the staff member believes they can contribute to the organization will be better able to place employees in altered roles satisfying to the staff member and resulting in a more effective outcome for the organization. We can overlook the opportunity to engage employees in discussions about the restructuring and move immediately to communicating decisions that have been made, but without consultation with them for fear of disagreement or discourse. Often, the employee is equally cognizant of the need for a shift in their job responsibilities and recognizes that they are not contributing as significantly as they could to the organization. By providing opportunities to discuss how the employee feels their strengths can benefit the organization and its new priorities, leaders can use the shifting environment to better position staff and increase employee satisfaction as well as goal achievement for the organization.

In moments of self-reflection, I have also noticed times when I became desensitized to restructuring in the organization because of experiencing multiple changes in a short period of time. I can remember thinking that the organization exhibited great adaptability and flexibility to regularly occurring shifts in priorities, but I also began to overlook the impact of the instability on employee retention and goal achievement.

Leaders of organizations experiencing frequent change can also ignore subtle nuances that are important to the employees impacted by the shifts—operational details, reporting lines, and even office space. I had to challenge myself to continue to engage the staff in dialogue around the fluctuating environment and to not neglect the impact of even the smallest changes on employees. Adaptability and flexibility must be balanced with sustainability and persistence in the organization.

As I think back over 20 years in Student Affairs and Higher Education, some of my most memorable work experiences do not involve direct interaction with students. Instead, the moments of significance involve modifications in the organizational structure. It is a concerning statement in a career focused on serving students and enhancing student learning that I would identify more meaning in how the organization dealt with change and was structured. It made me think about George Kuh's work regarding student engagement and collegiate quality (2003, 2009).

The first feature of student engagement often receives the most focus—the amount of time and energy students spend in educationally purposeful activities, but the second feature is particularly relevant for this discussion. The second critical feature of student engagement is how the institution deploys and organizes its resources to get students to participate in activities linked to student learning. By recognizing organizational restructuring and change as an opportunity to better serve students, leaders are able to facilitate meaningful conversations among employees about the arrangement of resources to achieve organizational goals instead of being unsettled by the disruption and change.

Dr. Amy Murphy
Dean of Students
Texas Tech University

Surviving organizational change requires a leader or manager with a sense of balance and an ability to handle oneself in the face of considerable conflict. In some cases, conflict so large-scale that it creates the potential for panic-stricken employees, students and parents, and intense emotions. While having an understanding of the potential generational diversity within a system can be helpful, having a steady hand and calm head through the rough waters of change is essential.

2. SURVIVING A DIFFICULT BOSS OR COLLEAGUE

If you have ever had a boss or colleague and wondered how they landed their role, and how long it would be until they were found out for their inexperience, incompetence or bullying behaviors, then you understand the impetus for this section on surviving a difficult boss or colleague. The capacity for leadership is one that few speak about, or prepare you for when you move into your first senior role. It is a shock to the system when you find yourself carrying others, or when they set their manipulative or abusive sights on you.

From a leadership perspective, we not only carry our own experiences, but those of our staff, who look to us to validate and affirm them. This calls to mind the classic fairytale by Hans Christian Andersen about two weavers who promise an emperor a new suit of clothes that is invisible to those who are unfit for their positions, stupid, or incompetent. In the *Emperor's New Clothes* (1837), the Honest Boy is unwilling to hold his tongue, calling out the truth that the Emperor is indeed naked, and has been tricked by the crafty weavers. This classic story helps us understand this workplace experience by reminding us how critical it is to be able to tell the truth as we see it, and how difficult it can be to buy in to a shared fairytale.

In his work, *The No Asshole Rule: Building a Civilized Workplace and Surviving One That Isn't* (2007), Stanford professor of business Robert Sutton, Ph.D., explores this phenomenon and helps us fortify against just such colleagues. He describes the need to lead up in the chapter aptly titled, "*When Assholes Reign*," and, while we pause a moment when using this kind of language in a book on leadership, Sutton shares his conviction that in some cases, no other descriptor will do. It is simply the best way to describe a bad boss or difficult colleague.

He describes strategies for surviving when the person above us, or to our left or right in the organization fits this description. He explores some concepts of reframing: "*hoping for the best, but expecting the worst, developing indifference and emotional detachment, looking for small wins, limiting your exposure, and building pockets of safety, support and sanity.*" (2007, pp. 125–151)

In reframing, the strategy is about changing one's mindset to reduce the damage that the situation might do. The reframing strategy of "hoping for the best, but expecting the worst" builds upon psychologist Martin Seligman's (2006) work on learned optimism. That is to say that we maintain optimism about our interactions with these people, while simultaneously maintaining a very low bar of expectation—so that our hopes are not dashed when they fail to behave as we wish they would. The challenge here, of course, is to avoid the potential paranoia, anxiety and hesitancy to action that are the normal reactions to dealing with a difficult boss. The key is developing a sense of equanimity, being both ready to be pleasantly surprised by a positive response while being aware of contingency plans if things don't go as well.

Another of the reframing strategies Sutton describes is "limiting your exposure." As you might guess, this strategy means exactly what it says: limiting the opportunities to stand toe-to-toe with this person means that you suffer less—shorter and technology-enabled meetings (dial-in or video conference) prove effective for limiting exposure. Again, the challenge becomes finding the middle ground of limiting one's exposure between being paralyzed by avoiding contact with the difficult boss and seeking out intentional fights, when a better alternative would be choosing the more balanced middle.

EXAMPLE FROM THE EXPERT— 10.2: LIFE'S TOO SHORT FOR CRAZY BOSSES!

This topic is particularly close to my heart having experienced workplace relationships where I needed to learn, and learn quickly, strategies for surviving a bully whose unfortunate position senior to me meant that I was a target of, or witness to, their bad behavior. A Gen Xer with high empathy, the days, weeks, and months spent under this person's thumb, and watching others suffering the same fate, took all of the fortifying strategies I could muster.

Early in my career I searched for strategies to survive these experiences. A close colleague told me that she would give her intellectual energy, but not her emotional energy, to the senior bully. Her strategy was to develop the indifference and emotional detachment described by Sutton. And, while I saw this strategy work for her for a while, it was clear that it took a toll on her emotionally and physically.

I found unexpected solace in Don Miguel Ruiz' book, *The Four Agreements* (1997). The four principles, or "agreements," that he describes in his work are agreements we make with ourselves that have helped me time and again when I found myself in the presence (or at the mercy) of a workplace bully. Ruiz' four agreements are: 1. *Be impeccable with your word*; 2. *Don't take anything personally*; 3. *Don't make assumptions*; 4. *Always do your best*. In my case, "always do your best" and "don't take anything personally" have been my salvation in workplace settings where bullies reign.

161

Bullies prey on our insecurities, and their behaviors seek to belittle and make us feel "less than." In always doing my best, I could reason with myself, asking, "Did you do your best here?" If the answer was yes, then I was able to rise above. The second agreement, "don't take anything personally," was a fitting reminder that this bad behavior had nothing to do with me and allowed me to resist the temptation to fall into despair about what of my own failings had resulted in me being persecuted by the bully.

Using the four agreements in this way, I utilize Sutton's (2010) strategies of *reframing*, by using these principles to avoid self-blame, and of *building pockets of safety, support and sanity*, by identifying a mantra that I could repeat again and again if I found myself in a difficult situation with this bully.

The final strategy, *finding small wins*, happened quite accidentally one day, shortly before the bully's departure from our institution. I found myself alone in the elevator with him, and he seemed to be mesmerized by something I was carrying. It wasn't until after we parted ways that I realized I'd been carrying Sutton's book, *"The No Asshole Rule,"* and had come face to face with the very person whose behavior had me reading it! I shared this story again and again with close colleagues—it was fun to feel that in some small way, I'd been able to tell him what I thought of him!

Poppy Fitch, M.A.
Ashford University

In Juan Camarena's Example from the Expert that follows, he stresses the universality of the need for status, power, and control in families and organizations, and notes that the ability to have influence within these systems is not predicated on status; indeed, it has everything to do with maintaining a clear sense of self.

EXAMPLE FROM THE EXPERT—
10.3: NAVIGATING A HOSTILE SYSTEM

I thought I knew what it was to lead. After all, I had successfully led teams of mental health clinicians at outpatient community mental health clinics for seven years, and had been praised and promoted many times over the course of my career. My supervisors, mentors, and coworkers valued me and did their best to stop me from moving into academia full time. They believed I was an effective leader and trusted me to make difficult decisions with a great deal of autonomy; they also predicted I would have a tough time wading through the muck of bureaucracy at a large state university. But I chose to leave my senior management position and jump into a new pond.

I had been a part-time lecturer for almost ten years when I decided to accept a full-time lecturer position in a multicultural graduate counseling program that I loved. I craved the academic schedule, having more time with students, and being more involved on the university campus. I also accepted a position as the Director of the program. So even though I was only a lecturer (bottom of the totem pole in academia), I now had a position which gave me access to the decision-makers in the department, college, and university-at-large. I felt fortunate to be given the opportunity, considering that I had not yet finished my doctorate degree.

It was during my first department faculty meeting when I understood that I was now a goldfish in a large pond with piranha, eels, and cuddle fish—that appeared friendly, but were actually the most dangerous. I came to understand the rules within each school of fish and I tried my best to abide by the unspoken rules that were a part of the pond. When I found myself getting caught up in the drama of the eels versus the piranhas, and was coming home every day to tell my partner about the latest cuddle fish who might be trying to poison me, I realized that I did not know how to lead from the bottom.

I realized that it's much easier to lead when you have high status within the overarching hierarchy. Since I was not a tenured professor, I needed to use another strategy to gain respect from my colleagues and advocate for my program. I made the decision to use my training as a family psychotherapist to inform how I would join and then interrupt the system (pond) I was now a part of. My greatest assets became bringing a calm demeanor and sense of internal balance to department meetings. Even when there was outright hostility taking place among piranhas and sharks, I made it a point to keep my emotional reactivity lowered and communicate in a clear and direct manner. I asked clarifying questions and often started sentences with affirmations of what had just been stated, and then asking for clarification on points I disagreed with.

After meetings, my colleagues would tell me privately that they appreciated my contributions and were glad that I was a part of the department. Within meetings, I could see that others were interested in my contributions and my perspective was valued. When that started to occur, I realized that many of the fish I perceived to be piranhas, were actually goldfish that acted like large fish with dangerous teeth.

The need for status, power, and control seem universal in families and organizations, but having influence in these systems comes from maintaining a solid sense of self. The more I've focused on my self-care, having a meaningful life outside of work, and creating emotional boundaries, the easier it has become to be a part of a murky pond. I've learned that I can be an influential leader from the bottom of the hierarchy, but it takes consistent interpersonal work to gain intrapersonal success.

Juan Camarena, Ph.D.
Program Director and Lecturer, Community Based Block
Co-Director, Center for Community Counseling and Engagement
San Diego State University

3. GRIEF AND LOSS IN THE WORKPLACE

When personal tragedy arrives in the workplace, it can be one of the most challenging leadership lessons we learn—and we learn it *on the job*. Core values become our salvation and we lean on them to both support the affected staff member and to address the ripple effect that our teams may experience. Serious illness, the death of a loved one, divorce, catastrophe, and acts of violence are just a few of the many examples of personal tragedy that we, and our teams, may bring with us to the workplace. Human Resources directs the oversight of the Family Medical Leave Act (FMLA) and the Americans with Disabilities (ADA) compliance in the handling of some of these examples. But, in navigating the day-to-day, direct supervisors become a critical source of support to both individuals and teams when tragedy strikes.

As in Chapter 4, our intention is not to turn leaders and managers into clinicians; however, having an understanding of the core concepts related to grief and loss help position us to be effective when navigating through such issues with our teams. Elisabeth Kübler-Ross pioneered the field of palliative care, hospice and end-of-life studies with her seminal work *On Death and Dying* (1969), where she first discussed the Kübler-Ross model. Here, she proposed what became widely known as the Five Stages of Grief and presented them as a pattern of adjustment. In her later work with Kessler, *On Grief and Grieving* (2005), Kübler-Ross explores the meaning of grief through the Five Stages, as previously described.

When understanding the stages of grief, it is important to realize there is no ideal time frame to work through the loss or trauma. Some people are able to return to their lives and schedules within a matter of days or weeks following a tragedy. Other people take months or years to work through the loss they must endure. Still others have complicated grief reactions that keep the person from returning to work or school, or connecting in meaningful relationships, and some contemplate suicide as the only way to be once again with the one they love. While a supervisor is in a better place to address grief and loss by understanding these stages, we must be cautious to not confuse the stages of grief with the personal experience of grief. As Polish American philosopher Alfred Korzybski wrote, "The map is not the territory" (Kendig, 1990, p. 299).

THE FIVE STAGES OF GRIEF

The five stages of grief as outlined by Kübler-Ross (1969, 2005 with Kessler) are Denial, Anger, Bargaining, Depression, and Acceptance. Denial may take many forms. You may find your employee exhibiting shock-like reactions such as fear, avoidance and confusion; all are common in this stage. In Denial, you may find that you or other team members seem to be more affected than the individual. Frustration, hostility, and anxiety are hallmarks of individuals moving through Anger. In this stage, hostility may be misplaced upon workplace issues unrelated to the trauma or tragedy. Supervisors and teammates will do well to understand this stage and offer additional grace to the individual while simultaneously balancing the health and vitality of the team. Kindness will go a long way in diffusing anger. Bargaining happens when the individual begins reaching out and sharing their story as a mechanism to support their search for meaning. For supervisors and colleagues, listening and validating is key at this stage.

The next stage that Kübler-Ross describes, Depression, may appear as helplessness, feelings of being overwhelmed, and intense sadness. At this stage, supervisors and colleagues can and should provide emotional support, as well as point the affected individual toward external resources, whether trusted friends and family, or professional support available

165

PUTTING IT INTO PRACTICE

through your Employee Assistance Program. These resources serve as important touchpoints as individuals move through this stage. Finally, at Acceptance, you will see the individual looking at options, making a new plan, and ultimately moving on and moving through the event.

Remember, the stages are not time bound or linear. This means that there is no "appropriate" amount of time for an individual to move from one stage to the next, and individuals may bounce from Denial to Bargaining to Anger and back to Denial. Owing to the lack of predictability inherent in this lack of linear progression, the day-to-day of the workplace may offer a welcome solace to the individual in its reliability. In any case, supervisors will need to support affected individuals as they make decisions about whether leaves of absence are necessary as they navigate the issue at hand, or if simple use of sick or other paid time off is sufficient.

Kübler-Ross' exploration of the Five Stages of Grief is undertaken through the lens of inevitable life changes that we all experience. The universality of these events make them a part of our common human experience. The notion that we can *check our personal lives at the office door* undermines this common experience and serves only to minimize the impact of such life changes on the individual, and their team.

Talking with a staff member that has suffered a tremendous loss such as a family death can be a daunting task. Supervisors should offer care, support, and empathetic listening. Beyond adopting this stance, the following is a list of suggestions you can offer to an employee who is grieving:

- Make a point to eat and sleep even if you are not hungry or tired.
- Keep up your daily routine as much as possible.
- Don't compare yourself to others; this is *your* grief.
- Take time to be by yourself if you need it, but don't isolate yourself.
- Don't think alcohol, drugs, food, sex, or spending money will help.
- Decide how you will remember the person you have lost; begin to write the story you will tell about them to others.
- Talk to family and friends.
- Read poetry or books.
- Seek spiritual support.
- Be patient with yourself.
- Engage in social activities.
- Join a support group.
- Exercise and eat good foods.
- Listen to music.
- Let yourself feel the grief.
- Take time to relax.

- Seek time with pets (Calvin and Hobbes "fuzz" therapy).
- Reconnect with friends and loved ones.

Below, two leaders—Jessica Riley, Associate Director of Disability Services at University of Denver, and Poppy Fitch, Associate Vice President of Student Affairs at Ashford University—weave together a compelling narrative of professional growth concurrent with and through personal tragedy. This critical story helps leaders to bridge the notion that we operate in a binary system of personal or professional, when the truth is that we are all some combination of the two—or "profersonals."

A PERSONAL NARRATIVE: LEADING THROUGH LOSS, WITH LOVE

Poppy:

Jessica transferred to my department as a highly recommended internal candidate from the Registrar's office at the University where we both worked. I looked forward to knowing her and learning about the ways she would bring her talents to support the students with disabilities who were served by our department. As a rapidly growing institution, the demand for our services was high. The department struggled with workload. I eagerly anticipated Jessica's contribution to the team. We began meeting weekly to orient her to the department and to get to know one another.

On our first meeting, Jessica broke down in tears. She shared that her father had been diagnosed with terminal cancer and that she would be his primary caretaker. I remember feeling so shocked—she seemed so young to be taking on this weighty responsibility. I wanted to help her, to offer some relief. And so began our relationship.

Jessica:

I went to work each morning, after making sure my father had eaten and taken his medication. It was hard to leave him, but he was insistent he did not want me to leave my job. He didn't want to be a burden in my life, or to hold me back in any way. So, I kept going; coming home from work to cook and clean—usually until late into the night. I was tired and burning the candle at both ends. At work, my emotions were always close to the surface. Student issues felt personal and critically important. I questioned every decision leadership made. I couldn't understand why no one else saw the problems. I took it on as my own personal mission to point out the error of our ways, every single one.

During one of my heartfelt pleas to Poppy, she asked me if I thought I was trying so hard to control things at work because there was so much in my life that I couldn't control. Of course, I broke down in tears. She had hit the nail on the head; this lesson was the first among many. I realized, much to my disappointment, I couldn't fix things for my students, I could only provide the tools and resources for them to navigate their own experience.

Poppy:

The technical elements of Jessica's situation meant that she would need flexibility to take her father to Doctors' appointments and that occasionally, she would need to stay home with him—easy enough. However, it was the emotional element of her situation that required real flexibility. I often noticed her displacing her feelings about losing her father onto things happening in the workplace. Everything was disproportionately intense, and our meetings often included her breaking down in tears. On the other hand, Jessica was a natural with her students and it was clear to me that she had the heart of a born counselor.

Shepherding Jessica through this time was the biggest leadership challenge I had faced. On the one hand, she was a talented and capable employee; on the other hand, she required a great deal of my energy and could sometimes be unpredictable in team meetings. When we talked about her future professional development (which, as a Millennial, came very early in her tenure) she often fell into tears. I remember once asking very directly, "Jess, you break down in tears each time we meet. Is this really about your job, or your professional development? What do you think is really happening here?"

Jessica:

The intense emotions didn't go away, but I learned to ask myself what my role was in each situation. I had always known that I had a tendency to get overly involved with my students—in this position and in others before. For the first time I felt like I had a point of reference from which to draw boundaries and that this, in the end, was a better way to serve my students. It was a turning point in my work as a counselor.

I had always seen my sensitivity as a weakness, but as I learned to draw healthier boundaries with my students—and with this realization—I fought to reconcile my empathy. After making some self-deflating remark in a team meeting, Poppy quickly challenged me; she pointed out that my sensitivity was what made me good at my job. She invited me to see myself through a different lens—to see my sensitivity as strength. In moments like that, I felt truly seen and valued.

I knew I was difficult to work with at times, but I also knew that my leadership team recognized my unique strengths. It may have been around this time that I was given more formal opportunities to mentor other employees and contribute to the development of our processes and policies. Looking back, I think some employers would have been focusing on my faults and looking to performance development plans. I feel so lucky that, instead, I had a boss who focused on my strengths and thoughtfully challenged me to grow. Had I not been recognized for my strengths, I could not have heard or coped with the challenging feedback.

Poppy:

Being with Jessica during this time in her life—her professional growth and her personal pain—challenged me to think about my core values as a leader. On the one hand, Jessica was clearly in pain and my high empathy might result in me overlooking some of the workplace concerns that she demonstrated. On the other hand, dismissing her poor behaviors and attributing them to her situation at home did a disservice to the rest of the team, as well as to Jessica.

I called upon my core values to lead me through this experience. I knew that what Jessica needed was compassion, and I worked to model that to the team. It wasn't always easy and sometimes I felt frustrated by being challenged, often in open forums, by Jessica. I also came to an awareness, for the first time, of generational influences in the workplace.

Jessica:

As my father's condition worsened, Poppy and I discussed FMLA. Ten days after I left work, my father passed away. No matter how much you think you are prepared for it, the grief is overwhelming. I threw myself into planning his memorial. My team at work volunteered to set up, cater, and clean up the reception. My family was stunned. I was overwhelmed with gratitude. It meant so much to have their support.

Months later, still grieving, I returned to work, emotions running high. Then, I had a conversation with Poppy that set my life and my career on a whole new path. True to form, I challenged the way the university was handling annual pay increases, pointing out that I was being short-changed. Poppy said to me, "There are other ways to progress professionally, Jessica. It doesn't make sense to me that you are not in a position of leadership on this team. Except that, well, it would be nice to go to a team meeting where I wasn't worried about you tearing us down." (Ouch.) "I'm not sure if it's because of personal circumstance or professional immaturity." (Double ouch.) "You are so positive with your students; I see it every day. It would be nice to see you bring more of that positivity to lifting up the team." I cried. It hurt. She was right. It was time for me to turn the page.

169

In that moment, my life changed. A weight was lifted. I still ask the hard questions. I still see when there is a better way, but now I can approach it from a solution-oriented perspective.

Poppy:

In the end, I found that approaching conversations with Jess with an equal balance of strength and kindness was most effective. When I felt frustrated with her in a team meeting, I would practice offering her grace, while still holding her accountable—mostly in private—for the behavior. Sometimes I used direct—and upon reflection, perhaps even harsh—lines of questioning in order to interrupt the "story" that Jess might be telling. One commitment that I made to her (and to the rest of my team) was that she could count on me to be authentic.

Learning from Jessica was one of the most powerful experiences of my professional life. I realized that as leaders, it is easy to put people into buckets—the "superstars" and the "poor performers." I realized that as employees, we're all a little bit of both. During this time, I thought a lot about my current supervisors and those I had encountered previously. I became more aware of myself and the ways I "showed up" in the workplace. And here, in this lesson with Jessica, I became certain of my commitment to lead with love.

Jessica:

Things quickly took off for me. I took a promotion and moved to a new city. Another promotion followed within the year. This past year, I changed schools to take the next step into an Assistant Director role. I am thankful for the mentor I still have in Poppy.

I recently tried to replicate the conversation that changed my life with one of my employees. It did not have quite the same effect. I realized that the crucial feedback does not land as well if it is not given from someone you trust. *Why did I trust Poppy enough to hear it? Because she recognized me, she saw me. It wasn't superficial. She saw what I was truly good at and helped me to see it. So, when she hit me with the hard stuff, I trusted her intentions. I was able to see the truth in what she was saying. I'm still growing as a leader, but I'm thankful to have a roadmap.*

CONCLUSION

In closing our exploration of leadership through the lens of these three scenarios—*Organizational Change, the Difficult Boss,* and *Grief and Loss*—let us revisit Chapter 4's quote from Carl Rogers (1961) who offers the following: "when someone understands how it feels and seems to be me, without wanting to analyze me or judge me, then I can blossom and grow in that climate" (p. 62). Our three Examples from the Experts demonstrate how to maneuver through the tides of change, both personal and professional, in ways that not only maintain our equilibrium, but also serve as a support to the "blossoming and growth" of our staff.

An unspoken concern of many supervisors are the challenges and threats to a peaceful department or work environment. These threats can be systemic, in terms of organizational change or restructuring, bad behavior on the part of leadership or colleagues, extreme personal circumstances, political wrangling in terms of appointments, departmental cliques and working within a stagnant or monarchical system. As with many themes in the book, the key to success lies in more fully understanding the motivations of the other person, system or politics before selecting the most effective approach to managing the situation.

DISCUSSION QUESTIONS

1. The authors explore the concept of organizational change against the backdrop of overall stability that institutions of higher education have traditionally provided. What is your experience with organizational change? How would you/have you and your teams respond(ed) if/when change was required of you?

2. Why do you think change is so difficult for people? Look to Bolman and Deal's (2013) frames (Table 10.1) and consider your own generational affiliation, and that of your employees. How do the examples given in this chapter match with your own experiences?

3. Give an example of a difficult boss you have worked with at a previous job. What techniques or approaches were helpful in mitigating conflict? How were you able to bring about change while working uphill against management?

4. In dealing with systemic or political issues in the office, it is often helpful to seek support and guidance from others. What are some examples where you sought support and reassurance from others to manage a difficult time?

5. While the goals of supervision most often focus on how to monitor or improve workplace performance, there are times when supervision becomes much more personal during a crisis event. Discuss some of the pros and cons of using a supervision session to offer support to an employee going through a difficult time or transition.

Just One Thing

Charles R. Minnick, Ph.D.
Vice President/Campus Director
Ashford University

I believe that one of the most important leadership traits is courage. Exceptional leadership is about focusing on what's really important among all other things. Sometimes that means having the courage to relentlessly pursue truth, even at the cost of personal pride, in service of building something everyone can be proud of. Courage does not mean the absence of fear, rather it means having the insight necessary to realize that something else is more important than the fear.

Afterword

TEN PRINCIPLES

Burning Man is a festival in Nevada that, on many levels, defies description; much like Steinbeck's famous opening quote describing Cannery Row as "a poem, a stink, a grating noise, a quality of light, a tone, a habit, a nostalgia, a dream," Burning Man exists like this. The gathering rises once a year out of the Black Rock Desert in the heat of August and early September on a dry lakebed about three hours north of Reno, Nevada. It's been going on for more than twenty years, with the first festival taking place on San Francisco's Baker Beach in 1986.

It is an intentional community based on the concept of gifting. No money changes hands at Burning Man and nothing is sold or purchased. Around 70,000 people join the community each year. Once the week comes to a close, the 100-foot plus wooden man is burned on Saturday night followed by the burning of the wooden temple structure on Sunday. It's a leave-no-trace experience. The lakebed reassumes its natural state as the participants leave to return to the "default world" until next year.

People come searching for something—a break from the everyday life, a chance to connect with other people, to interact with art, to party, to run naked in the sunshine, to seek a higher spiritual connection, to get drunk, to take illegal drugs, to listen to music, check an experience off a bucket list, or ride on mystical art cars shaped like pirate ships and giant sharks. There is no shortage of things to do at Burning Man. Everyone finds what they are looking for at Black Rock City. In the end, the playa provides.

So, why end this book about leadership, management and supervision with a discussion of Burning Man? We believe there is a connection between the book subject and the ten principles written in 2004 as guidelines for the event. They were not created to tell people how to act, but rather as a reflection of the community's culture as it evolved over time. These principles offer some wisdom, we believe, for those looking to build their own intentional communities within the college and university settings.

1. RADICAL INCLUSION

Anyone may be a part of Burning Man. We welcome and respect the stranger. No prerequisites exist for participation in our community.

Everyone is welcome. Diversity is the hallmark of this festival. From the twenty-something glitter-covered sparkle ponies to the wise old mystics and healers in their eighties; Millennials, Gen Xer's, Boomers and Matures wander the lakebed playa together, forming a diverse tapestry of light, music, love, letting go and spiritual awakenings. From the youngest to the oldest, from all around the world, everyone is welcome.

As those who attend Burning Man quickly learn on their first visit, a cacophony of sounds, tastes, cultures, art, costumes, mutant vehicles and people all come together under the watchful eye of the man in the center of the village. Each individual camp is made up of people with unique strengths and weaknesses. Camps work together well when they appreciate these differences and encourage each other, stepping in to help when an area of need is identified.

The lesson here for managers and leaders working with staff is the power of diversity. Chapter 5 explored diversity in terms of assessing and appreciating the different personalities and ways of interacting that people bring to a task. Instead of viewing difference as out of step, off-mission or ineffective, managers and leaders should seek to capitalize on the diversity of spirit, approaches to problem-solving, and the ability to support and encourage others and those who have passion and commitment to the work.

EXAMPLE FROM THE EXPERT— 11.1: USING DIFFERENCE

I was the director of counseling at Western Kentucky University for seven years in the late 2000s. One of the lessons I learned from working there was the power inherent in having a diverse clinical staff. Some college counseling centers exclusively hire one kind of clinical staff, say psychologists, and the services offered through the center tend to be fairly consistently practiced from that perspective.

At WKU, we had a diverse staff of individuals from various walks of life. Some were trained as psychologists, others as master-level therapists. Some specialized in working with students working through a sexual assault, others worked best with those recovering from an eating disorder, substance abuse problem or suicidal thoughts. We had a nice mixture of generations in our office, covering all four of the generations we explore in this book. There was a robust and vibrant internship and practicum program that brought new and younger staff onto our team, sometimes challenging the way we approached care. The diversity of our staff was our strength.

From a management standpoint, some were sticklers to details and responded quickly to requests for reports or information I needed to track as the director. Others excelled at their clinical work and struggled more with the paperwork and administrative tasks. Some were early morning people and arrived before the office was scheduled to be open. Others stayed late and worked into the evenings, offering programs that suited the students' schedules and time frames. Our office worked well because everyone was different. Each person was a part of the center and contributed their strengths and weaknesses to the overall good of the service we offered.

As I look back at my time leading this diverse group of clinicians, I'd like to hope that one thing I did well was appreciating and encouraging this diversity. Meeting the staff where they were and trying my best to understand how they approached problems and their work from their individual perspective. In this way, everyone contributed to the overall mission of the department.

Brian Van Brunt, Ed.D.
The NCHERM Group

2. GIFTING

Burning Man is devoted to acts of gift giving. The value of a gift is unconditional. Gifting does not contemplate a return or an exchange for something of equal value.

One of the hardest things for people new to Burning Man to understand is the gifting economy at the gathering. There is no money at Burning Man. You cannot buy anything during the festival with the exceptions of ice,

175

coffee and tea at the center camp. You have what you have brought into the desert—water, food, camping supplies. Anything you need to live for a week has to be brought in.

A gifting economy is different from a barter economy. Gifting is about giving something with no expectation of return. People gift food and drinks or services. Well-known camps at Burning Man include the French Quarter that gifts gumbo each night. Human Carcass Wash camp gifts the odd, and not-for-the-shy experience of going through a human car-wash bathing experience with soap and many hands washing your dust-covered naked body. Another camp offers grilled cheese and Pabst Blue Ribbon beer. Gifts are random, spontaneous and given with no expectation of being paid back.

In the office setting, the idea of supervision and leadership often takes on this approach of caring for the professional development and career of the employees under your care. While supervision often focuses on the here-and-now behaviors that contribute to the overall effectiveness of the department, sometimes supervision is about caring for the person sitting across from you in a way apart from their future at your particular college or university. You may encourage a staff member to go to a conference that will help them network and find greater opportunities for growth and development. Sometimes the best supervision sessions put aside the current issues related to work and focus instead on the more pressing needs the employee is struggling with in their personal life. In this way, good supervision is a gift that has no expectation of return. Good supervisors, leaders and managers give their wisdom, care and guidance with no expectations of return or reward.

3. DECOMMODIFICATION

In order to preserve the spirit of gifting, our community seeks to create social environments that are unmediated by commercial sponsorships, transactions, or advertising. We stand ready to protect our culture from such exploitation. We resist the substitution of consumption for participatory experience.

For those who haven't experienced Burning Man before, it can come as a shock to spend a week away from the pervasive marketing and consumerism that is so prevalent in American culture. There is no sponsorship of Burning Man, no billboards or signs, no logos, advertisements or pressure to buy something. To this end, participants become free to interact with each other without currency. Money doesn't exchange hands for services. There is striving to create an equal playing field for everyone in attendance. There is no special access or services based on class, money or social standing.

One of the most memorable sights and experiences at Burning Man are the art cars that travel about the playa. These mutant vehicles used to be cars, golf carts, buses, trucks and semis. Now there is a giant pirate ship creating dance parties with large speakers, a 25-foot-high motorized toilet bowl the size of a tennis court, a shark with seating in its belly, an octopus shooting fire or a giant metal scorpion. There is no sight in the world like the art cars of Burning Man lit up all neon-bright, some shooting balls of flame, driving around the darkness of the playa. The amazing thing about the art cars is there is no schedule, no buying a ticket to get on board. A vehicle stops and you ask to get on. There is no telling where you will end up or when it will stop. There is no money exchanged. Everyone is able to access the experience, regardless of age, cultural background, or finances.

This idea comes into the workplace and to leadership through the lens of creating equal opportunities and connections for everyone in a department. While there is a temptation for any supervisor, leader or manager to have favorite employees, we must strive to treat our employees with the same sense of fairness and access. Being a good leader or manager requires allowing each employee an opportunity to share their ideas, work on projects that are meaningful to them and to not experience bias or favoritism from a department head or boss.

4. RADICAL SELF-RELIANCE

Burning Man encourages the individual to discover, exercise and rely on his or her inner resources.

This is one of our favorites. At the heart of self-reliance is an idea that overlaps well with the existential psychology movement—this idea of taking responsibility for your actions and living in a way that is intentional. At Burning Man, this concept means that each person is responsible for making sure they have the things they need for survival. Before asking a question, people are encouraged to explore whether or not they have the ability to find that answer on their own. This isn't to avoid connection to others or leaning on the larger community, rather it is an acknowledgement that the community itself is stronger if everyone first takes responsibility for their actions and is intentional with their actions.

It is a favorite because it encourages people—both in the middle of Black Rock City in Nevada as well as those working at colleges and universities— to take responsibility for their own behavior and find a solution to the

177

obstacle in front of them. It encourages staff to be active in problem identification and solving. Rather than complaining, becoming frustrated, blaming other people, becoming hopeless or lost, radical self-reliance encourages staff to take personal responsibility in both the identification and solution phase when a problem exists. This may require asking for extra resources, learning more about the nature of the obstacle, advocating for a new, innovative process or adjusting the original goals (if possible). All of these begin with the employee rather than the supervisor.

The manager's or leader's role then becomes instilling a sense of personal responsibility, mindfulness, attention to surroundings and an empowerment to identify and solve problems. This becomes harder when a director or department head is involved in micro-managing the employees' work or requires oversight and sign-off on relatively mundane tasks. Creating a team of radically self-reliant employees means having a team that always brings to your attention some ideas for a solution along with the problem.

EXAMPLE FROM THE EXPERT— 11.2: THE LOOP

Recently, I had a conversation with my supervisor about how he had perceived my attitude at work. I have the privilege of working from home and live over 500 miles from our main office. This arrangement works well for me as I have always struggled to keep a traditional 9–5 workday and much of my work is project-driven and involves traveling all around the country. One of the downsides of working from home is often feeling "out of the loop" on issues or projects that other staff talk about on a daily basis.

The problem came up when I complained about feeling unprepared to contribute to a project I was expected to be working on with another person in the office. I received an email explaining that my attitude wasn't what it needed to be on the project.

After this email, I took a few days to reflect on the situation. I felt justified with my complaint, as I had not been included on other communications about the project. However, the issue at hand wasn't so much the project, but more my perceived attitude about the project. After a few days of cooling off, I was able to get into a better headspace about how to be more radically self-reliant when it came to issues in the home office that I found myself out of touch around. In the following months, I became better about asking questions, and when I didn't have the information I needed to move forward on a project, instead of complaining, I sought out that information I needed to get back "into the loop."

The challenge for many of us is taking that personal responsibility after a corrective action and to examine our behavior in a different light. Asking ourselves how we can be part of the solution rather than complaining about the situation. Identifying the initial problem is important, but it is more important to come to the table with a solution.

Brian Van Brunt, Ed.D.
The NCHERM Group

5. RADICAL SELF-EXPRESSION

Radical self-expression arises from the unique gifts of the individual. No one other than the individual or a collaborating group can determine its content. It is offered as a gift to others. In this spirit, the giver should respect the rights and liberties of the recipient.

Burning Man is known for its crazy art projects and the colorful, whimsical and sometimes salacious costumes worn by those in attendance. Everyone is encouraged to share their thoughts, feelings and emotions through artistic expression: a participant dressed up like a giant penis jumping on a trampoline; a giant temple structure where people come and share their memories of loved ones and seek spiritual renewal in their faith; a long-haired man in a lawn chair reading Ginsberg's famous poem *Howl* into a megaphone outside a line of porta-potties early one morning—a favorite memory. Whatever you want to express, it is encouraged within the community.

There are clearly some exceptions in this application in the workplace. Yet, the underlying concept of expressing our individual thoughts, ideas and emotions, rather than avoiding sharing these, remains a useful one for managers to consider. While it can be difficult in conversation for a director or supervisor to listen and acknowledge that an employee is unhappy or frustrated, it is better this way than have those feelings held inside and left to fester and recirculate among the office staff. Setting up supervision with a clear expectation that the supervisor wants to hear the difficult things as well as the good things is a way to get staff to express their feelings and emotions about their work.

Likewise, leadership and management should encourage employees to share novel and innovative ways to look at problems and brainstorm potential solutions. We are reminded of the old saying, "If you always do what you've always done, you'll always get what you always got." A workplace is better when diverse ideas are shared and problems are explored with openness and curiosity. Solutions should be creative and foster a sense of community and shared vision.

6. COMMUNAL EFFORT

Our community values creative cooperation and collaboration. We strive to produce, promote and protect social networks, public spaces, works of art, and methods of communication that support such interaction.

A city of 70,000 people, the size of Portland, Maine, rises out of Black Rock Desert each year and then returns back into dust from where it once came. This happens through a powerful coming together of will and effort from the community. No one person makes Burning Man, rather the group coming together to reach our common goals. This process, like any other process of creation, is not without its growing pains and difficulties. Each year, different problems manifest that present challenges to the builders and those who participate.

From the outside, many see Burning Man as a hedonistic debauchery that takes place in the desert each year with nudity, sex, drunkenness, illegal drugs—essentially, a nonstop seven-day rave. And this is true. These are all things someone can find at Burning Man, but it is not what Burning Man is all about. The negative media coverage and rumors around the illegal drug activities draw local law enforcement, and the potential for arrest rises. Safety concerns exist each year in terms of 70,000 people camping in one of the most inhospitable environments on earth. Yet, the community comes together and sees its way through these difficulties, whether they be weather, law enforcement, the high price ($380–$800), the competitive ticket lottery or the growing number of participants that come to watch the spectacle rather than participate as part of the community (commonly known as plug-and-play camps).

Supervisors and directors, leaders and managers, have similar challenges to bring together a diverse work force, full of generational differences—the potential for misunderstanding or frustrations by employees who feel they are being treated unfairly or with bias. Budgets decrease and working conditions become difficult with little or no chance of raises or the ability to attend conferences or receive other professional funds for growth. So the challenge exists for the department head or boss to build a sense of community that can weather these storms.

As we outlined in Chapter 6, this building of a community works better when the leadership of the department spends its time and treasure to create professional development events and staff retreats dedicated to bringing a team together. These efforts improve communication, help employees learn about each other and improve their ability to empathize and work productively with those around them. As we've mentioned, this isn't always about money and having the budget to take a staff retreat to a luxury location; it *can* be, but it's really the ability to carve out the time and effort to bring the staff together and build a positive community.

7. CIVIC RESPONSIBILITY

We value civil society. Community members who organize events should assume responsibility for public welfare and endeavor to communicate civic responsibilities to participants. They must also assume responsibility for conducting events in accordance with local, state and federal laws.

Burning Man brings together a large number of diverse participants from around the world with the common goal of spending time together as part of an intentional community. This community seeks to put a positive, karmic vibe back into the universe. The community comes to appreciate art and each other. It is a chance to disconnect from technology (if you so choose) and to remember the power of a shared experience with others looking for a deeper connection.

Many come to Burning Man as a kind of touchstone or recharging event before returning to the other 51 weeks of the year in the "default world." It becomes a returning home for those who may not have had a supportive or caring home life. It becomes a chance to reaffirm the values of caring for other human beings and seeing the interconnection we share with each other. It's the true meaning of namaste—pausing to acknowledge the divinity within everyone, allowing our souls to briefly meet.

So how does this relate to the office environment? It's the idea of creating a larger goal for the department. Exploring, as a group, how we can come together to work towards a larger social goal. This could be pooling funds from around the office to give back to a good cause in the community, identifying ways to expand the service offered to students to reach beyond what is simply required in order to meet the spirit of our intentions, and so on.

As we discussed in Chapter 4, the idea of positive psychology and altruism helps support this concept. When people come together to give back to others, it creates an after effect of caring and support that makes people feel genuinely good about themselves in a lasting way. When this effort is coordinated through a collaborative project in an office, it has a positive effect on morale and collaboration that can drift over into office projects and productivity.

EXAMPLE FROM THE EXPERT— 11.3: THE GIFT THAT KEEPS ON GIVING

During my time as the director of counseling at Western Kentucky University, I had the privilege of being part of a group effort to support some families in need during the holidays. The director of testing worked with a local family at a school in Bowling Green and we coordinated gifts for Christmas. We all took a part of the list and came together to purchase toys, clothes, school supplies and other treats to make their holiday a better one. We had no illusions that we were fixing anything for the family long-term, but we knew that we made this one family's holiday a better one.

The benefit here was even more powerful for the staff than the family. It brought us together to do something kind and charitable for others. Even though most of our work was about helping people through therapy, the pulling together each holiday as a staff to support the family was something that was a memorable and palpable way to work together and strengthen our bond.

Brian Van Brunt, Ed.D.
The NCHERM Group

8. LEAVING NO TRACE

Our community respects the environment. We are committed to leaving no physical trace of our activities wherever we gather. We clean up after ourselves and endeavor, whenever possible, to leave such places in a better state than when we found them.

Burning Man bills itself as a leave-no-trace experience. What you pack into the city is packed out at the end. Garbage is disposed of at locations between Black Rock City and Reno at various trash stops, often run by

Native American families on tribal land. While there is always some debate each year concerning the positive versus negative impact of the event on the local community, overall the festival provides a boon of business along the drive in, and considerable tax revenue to the surrounding communities. We strive to leave the land and people better than we found them.

The concept plays out in the desert through the oddly named concept of MOOP. This stands for Matter Out Of Place. The idea is that no one brings materials that are easily swept away by the wind and environment of the desert. Things like feather boas, beanbag chairs filled with those little styrofoam balls and poorly attached bits of paper are all frowned upon at the event. A large trash fence encircles the city in order to catch any stray items that have blown away from a camp or careless burner. All participants are encouraged to spend four hours picking up MOOP during their time at the event. Camps are graded after the burn to praise or shame their compliance with the leave-no-trace approach.

While it would be nice if a workplace office shared some of Burning Man's ideology on recycling and keeping track of trash, the point here for supervisors and managers is found in the phrase "we clean up after ourselves." Good supervisors and directors don't leave unfinished problems or issues lying around the office. They seek to address problems as they occur and actively avoid the temptation to let someone else pick up the pieces of a failed project or communication failure. If there is an opportunity to make something better, to address a behavior that is out of place or smooth out an interaction that is going badly, good managers and leaders ultimately see themselves as responsible for addressing these problems and not leaving them for someone else to deal with at the trash fence.

It is also a hope here that this becomes a parallel process for employees, who see a manager or leader addressing issues rather than leaving problems unsolved. Trash has a way of gathering unchecked unless there is someone diligently maintaining the grounds. When a supervisor cares for an office well, they address problems and teach their subordinates to follow in their footsteps.

9. PARTICIPATION

Our community is committed to a radically participatory ethic. We believe that transformative change, whether in the individual or in society, can occur only through the medium of deeply personal participation. We achieve being through doing. Everyone is invited to work. Everyone is invited to play. We make the world real through actions that open the heart.

183

There are no watchers at Burning Man. Everyone is part of the spectacle. Each person and camp plays a role in making the entire event a success. From the fur-lined flatbed truck decorated with six-foot glowing mushrooms offering partygoers rides around the playa to those who serve ice, coffee, tea and lemonade in center camp, everyone contributes. Everyone is part of the event.

In the office setting, it is equally important to ensure everyone is part of the team and participates. This can be difficult since everyone has a different comfort level in terms of group events, office activities and tolerance for individual differences in the office. It isn't realistic that everyone likes everyone else, but an expectation is that everyone plays their own unique part, and respects the parts of others in the overall office gestalt.

If there is an employee left out of the office group, it is the role of an attentive supervisor or director to attend to this and attempt to connect the person into the larger office. The challenge here is finding the place that they fit while respecting the individuality and uniqueness of each person's abilities and comfort level in being part of the overall group. Are there places where the person who is distant can be given tasks that are within their comfort level that will help them shine in the larger social structure?

10. IMMEDIACY

Immediate experience is, in many ways, the most important touchstone of value in our culture. We seek to overcome barriers that stand between us and a recognition of our inner selves, the reality of those around us, participation in society, and contact with a natural world exceeding human powers. No idea can substitute for this experience.

One thing that Burning Man brings into focus for many participants is a sense of being bombarded with the sheer volume of sensations and experiences that all seem to occur simultaneously. "Overwhelming" doesn't quite capture the number of people, camps, hugs, colors, smells, music, fireball explosions, nakedness, neon, love and energy that spins and bangs around the playa like a dozen loose pinballs smacking against the machine's bumpers, spinners and targets. Paradoxically, this overwhelming of the senses creates a level of focus on the here-and-now. You become more aware of what is right in front of you, and attend to that rather than trying to keep up with the impossible task of trying to do everything, see everything.

A final skill that is helpful for a leader or manager to develop is the ability to attend mindfully to the here-and-now moments that occur in the office.

A group of employees is almost always a temporary arrangement, shifting and changing, as complex systems are known to do. While there is a value in strategic planning, reviewing goals, assessing productivity and creating positive communication and collaboration, there is no better way to end this book than to stress the power in a supervisor stopping by an employee's desk and asking them how their day is going. Attend in a mindful way to the people who work in your department and nurture the relationships through caring, kindness and, ultimately, love.

Just One Thing

Dr. Chip Reese
Assistant Vice President for Student Affairs & Dean of Students
Columbus State University

The One Thing - listen! Bill Newman said, "Successful people tend to make decisions quickly and change them rarely." You must understand your institutional policies and the State and Federal laws that apply to your area. With this information you can make timely and solid, policy-based decisions when students, parents, faculty, staff, and others set a problem on your desk. However, that is not the One Thing; policy and law knowledge simply puts you in a position so you can execute the One Thing in a calm, thoughtful and unemotional manner.

The One Thing - listen! Become an intentional listener. You will soon find there are few situations that will be completely new to your office. You will have a tendency to rush to the end of a good story, because you know where this train is going. I cannot stress enough how important it is to allow people to tell their story. In the telling, many times they will find their own answer. Of course, there will be times when you cannot deliver the resolution they desire, but you listened. The one thing people really want when they walk into your office: To be heard.

References

Ahlfinger, N., & Esser, J. (2001). Testing the groupthink model: Effects of promotional leadership and conformity predisposition. *Journal of Social Behavior and Personality, 29(1)*, 31–42.

Alexander, A. (2011, April 11). Four infographics about online trends, internet usage and social media. Retrieved from: http://ansonalex.com/technology/4-infographics-about-online-trends-internet-usage-and-social-media

Andersen, H. C. (1837). *Fairy tales told for children. First collection.* Copenhagen: C.A. Reitzel.

Arum, R., & Roksa, J. (2011). *Academically adrift: Limited learning on college campuses.* Chicago: University of Chicago Press.

ASME-ITI (2010). A Risk Analysis Standard for Natural and Man-Made Hazards to Higher Education Institutions. Association Society of Mechanical Engineers (ASME), Innovative Technologies Institute (ITI).

Besley, A. C. (2002). Foucault and the turn to narrative therapy. *British Journal of Guidance & Counselling, 30(2)*, 125–143.

Bock, L. (2015). Google's 10 secrets for transforming your team and your workplace, Fortune 100's best companies to work for. *Fortune, 171(4)*, 136–138.

Bok, D. C. (2013). *Higher education in America.* Princeton, NJ: Princeton University Press.

Boldt, R. M., & Mosak, H. H. (1998). Understanding the storyteller's story: Implications for therapy. *Journal of Individual Psychology, 54(4)*, 495–510.

Bolman, L. G., & Deal, T. E. (2013). *Reframing organizations: Artistry, choice, & leadership.* Hoboken, NJ: John Wiley & Sons.

Bradberry, T., & Greaves, J. (2009). *Emotional Intelligence 2.0.* San Diego, CA: TalentSmart.

Clifton, D., Anderson, E., & Schreiner, L. (2006). *StrengthsQuest: Discover and develop your strengths in academics, career, and beyond*. New York: Gallup Press.

Close, H. T. (1998). *Metaphor in psychotherapy: Clinical applications of stories and allegories*. Atascadero, CA: Impact Publishers.

Colvin, G. (2015). Personal Bests, Fortune 100's best companies to work for. *Fortune, 171(4)*, 106–110.

Corey, G. (2001). *Theory and practice of counseling and psychotherapy* (6th edn.). Belmont, CA: Brooks/Cole Thompson Learning.

Covey, S. M. R. (2006). *The speed of trust: The one thing that changes everything*. Sydney: Simon & Schuster.

Covey, S. R. (1990). *The seven habits of highly effective people*. London: The Free Press.

Csíkszentmihályi, Mihály (1990). *Flow: The psychology of optimal experience*. New York: Harper & Row.

Csíkszentmihályi, Mihály, & Csíkszentmihályi, Isabella Selega (Eds.) (1988). *Optimal Experience: Psychological studies of flow in consciousness*. Cambridge: Cambridge University Press.

Diener, E., & Diener, C. (1996). Most people are happy. *Psychological Science, 3*, 181–185.

Emmons, R. A., & Crumpler, C. A. (2000). Gratitude as a human strength: Appraising the evidence. *Journal of Social & Clinical Psychology, 19*, 56–69.

Farson, R. (1997). *Management of the absurd: Paradoxes in leadership*. New York: Simon & Schuster.

Fry, R. (2015). Millennials surpass Gen Xers as the largest generation in U.S. labor force, Fact Tank: News in the Numbers, Pew Research Center. Retrieved from: www.pewresearch.org/fact-tank/2015/05/11/millennials-surpass-gen-xers-as-the-largest-generation-in-u-s-labor-force/

Generations in History (2015). Retrieved from: www.lifecourse.com/assets/files/gens_in_history(1).pdf

Greenleaf, R. (1977). *Servant leadership—a journey into the nature of legitimate power and greatness*. Mahwah, NJ: Paulist Press.

Gronbach, K. W. (2008). *The Age Curve*. New York: AMACOM.

Haidt, J. (2000). The positive emotion of elevation, *Prevention & Treatment, 3*.

Harter, J. K., Schmidt, F. L., Killham, E. A., & Asplund, J. W. (2008). Q12® Meta-Analysis, Gallup. Retrieved from: https://strengths.gallup.com/private/resources/q12meta-analysis_flyer_gen_08%2008_bp.pdf

Hirsch, S., & Kummerow, J. (1989). *Lifetypes*. New York: Warner Books.

Keirsey, D. (1998). *Please understand me II: Temperament, character, intelligence.* Del Mar, CA: Prometheus Nemesis Books.

Keirsey, D., & Bates, M. M. (1978). *Please understand me: Character & temperament types.* Del Mar, CA: Prometheus Nemesis Books.

Kendig, M. (1990). *Alfred Korzybski: Collected writings, 1920-1950.* Englewood, NJ: Institute of General Semantics.

Kopp, R. R. (1995). *Metaphor therapy.* New York: Brunner/Mazel.

Kroeger, O., & Thuesen, J. M. (1988). *Type Talk.* New York: Dell Publishing.

Kübler-Ross, E. (1969). *On Death and Dying.* New York: Macmillan.

Kübler-Ross, E., & Kessler, D. (2005). *On grief and grieving: Finding the meaning of grief through the five stages of loss.* London: Simon & Schuster.

Kuh, G. D. (2003). What we're learning about student engagement from NSSE: Benchmarks for effective educational practices. *Change: The Magazine of Higher Learning, 35(2),* 24–32.

Kuh, G. D. (2009). The national survey of student engagement: Conceptual and empirical foundations. *New Directions for Institutional Research, 2009(141),* 5–20.

Lopez, Shane J. (2014). *Making hope happen: Create the future you want for yourself and others.* New York: Simon & Schuster.

Malcolm, D. (2005). *A whole new ball game: A close-up look at diversity, racism, sexism, affirmative action, cultural pluralism & the unfinished business remaining in twenty-first century America.* Fairfield, CT: Aslan Publishing.

McKnight, J., Asset-Based Community Development Institute: Northwestern University. (2008). Retrieved from http://www.abcdinstitute.org/docs/ A%20Basic%20Guide%20to%20ABCD%20Community%20 Organizing(3).pdf

Meloy, J. R., & Mohandie, K. (2014). Assessing threats by direct interview of the violent true believer. In J. R. Meloy & J. Hoffmann (Eds.), *The international handbook of threat assessment* (pp. 388–398). New York: Oxford University Press.

Myers, D. G. (2000). The funds, friends, and faith of happy people. *American Psychologist, 55,* 56–67.

Nydell, M. (1996). *Understanding Arabs: A guide for Westerners.* Yarmouth, ME: Intercultural Press.

Nylund, D. (2000). *Treating Huckleberry Finn: A new narrative approach to working with kids diagnosed ADD/ADHD.* San Francisco: Jossey-Bass.

O'Connor, T. S. (1999). Climbing mount purgatory: Dante's cure of souls and narrative family therapy. *Pastoral Psychology, 47(6),* 445–457.

Pink, D. (2005). *A whole new mind: Why right-brainers will rule the future*. New York: Riverhead Books.

Rath, T. (2007). *Strengths 2.0*. New York: Gallup Press.

Rath, T., & Conchie, B. (2009). *Strengths based leadership*. New York: Gallup Press.

Ray, J., & Kafka, S. (2014). Life in college matters for life after college. Gallup, Inc. Retrieved from: www.gallup.com/poll/168848/life-college-matters-life-college.aspx?version=print

Roberts, R. (2007, June 11). Dan Pink on 'How half your brain can save your job'. Podcast. Retrieved from: www.econtalk.org/archives/2007/06/dan_pink_on_how.html

Rogers, C. R. (1961). *On becoming a person*. New York: Houghton Mifflin.

Rogers, C. R. (1980). *A way of being*. New York: Houghton Mifflin.

Ruiz, D. M. (1997). *The four agreements*. San Rafael, CA: Amber-Allen Publishing.

Ryan, R. M., & Deci, E. L. (2000). Self-determination theory and the facilitation of intrinsic motivation, social development, and well-being. *American Psychologist, 55*, 68–78.

Sanders, Tim (2002). *Love is the killer app: How to win business and influence friends*. New York: Three Rivers Press.

Seligman, M. E. (2006). *Learned optimism: How to change your mind and your life*. New York: Vintage.

Seligman, M., Steen, T., Nansook, P., & Peterson, C. (2005) Positive Psychology Progress: Empirical Validation of Interventions. *Tidsskrift for Norsk Psykologforening, 42(10)*, 874–884.

Snyder, B. (2015). Half of us have quit our job because of a bad boss. *Fortune* magazine. Retrieved from: http://fortune.com/2015/04/02/quit-reasons/

Strauss, W., & Howe, N. (1997). *The fourth turning: An American prophesy*. New York: Broadway Books.

Strauss, W., & Howe, N. (2003). *Millennials go to college*. Washington, D.C.: American Association of Collegiate Registrars and Admissions Officers.

Stringer, E. T. (1999). *Action research* (2nd edn.). Thousand Oaks, CA: Sage Publications.

Sutton, R. (2007). *The No Asshole Rule: Building a civilized workplace and surviving one that isn't*. New York: Business Plus.

Tan, Chade-Meng (2012). *Search inside yourself: The unexpected path to achieving success, happiness (and world peace)*. New York: HarperCollins.

Thomson, L. (1998). *Personality type: An owner's manual*. Boston, MA: Shambala Books.

Toossi, M. (2012). Employment outlook: 2010–2020. Bureau of Labor Statistics. Retrieved from: www.bls.gov/opub/mlr/2012/01/art3full.pdf

Van Brunt, B. (2007). *Thematic apperception test: Administration and interpretation.* Prescott, AZ: Borrego.

Van der Meer, B., & Diekhuis, M. (2014). Collecting and assessing information for threat assessment. In J. R. Meloy & J. Hoffmann (Eds.), *The international handbook of threat assessment* (pp. 54–66). New York: Oxford University Press.

Ward, B., & Bloom, A. (2006). *The wisdom of the desert fathers.* Collegeville, MN: Cistercian Publications.

White, M. (1988–9). *The externalizing of the problem and the re-authoring of lives and relationships.* Dulwich Centre Newsletter (Summer), 5–28.

White, M., & Epston, D. (1990). *Narrative means to therapeutic ends.* New York: WW Norton & Company.

Zimmerman, J. L., & Beaudoin, M. (2002). Cats under the stars: A narrative story. *Child and Adolescent Mental Health, 7(1)*, 31–40.

Index

Note: Page numbers in *italics* are for tables.

motivation 7
Murphy, A. 157–9
Myers, D. G. 64
Myers-Briggs Type Inventory (MBTI) 72, 74, 81–6

narrative approach 51, 52, 57–63
Newman, B. 186
Nieto-Senour, M. 55–6

open-door policy 112–13
open-ended, circular questions 111
optimism, learned 160–1
organizational change 155–9

parents, of Millenials 18, 21
participation 183–4
Pattenaude, R. 39–30
perceptive individuals 83, 84
person-centered approach 51, 52–6
personal life 8–9
personality 150–1; assessment *see* Myers-Briggs Type Inventory (MBTI)
Piersa, W. 73–6
Pink, D. 4–5
politics 10–11
positive psychology 51, 52, 63–8, 182
privilege of leadership 5–6
productivity 6
professional development 90–2, 95–101

rapport, in supervisory relationship 106–9
Rath, T. 76, 77
Reese, C. 186
reflection 6; self- 89, 117, 153
relationships 3–15
resistance to change 138, 142–4
respect 9–12, 32, 117, 119
responsibility 8–9

right-brained approaches 4
Riley, J. 167–70
Robinson, K. 79–81
Rogers, C. R. 52, 53, 54, 170–1
Roksa, J. 156
role models 71
Roosevelt, T. 73
Ross, R. 111
Ruiz, D. M., Four Agreements 161–2
Ryan, R. M. 64

Salter, S. 114–17
Sanders, T. 5
Saracino, E. 32
Schultz, H. 5
Scott, P. S. 35–7
Search Inside Yourself program 5
self, sense of 162, 164
self-assessment tools 71–2; Gallup StrengthsFinder 2.0 72, 74, 76–7; Myers-Briggs Type Inventory (MBTI) 72, 74, 81–6
self-awareness 5, 70–89
self-disclosure 108–9
self-expression 179–80
self-reflection 89, 117, 153
self-reliance 177–9
Seligman, M. 52, 65, 160
sense of purpose 67
sensing individuals 82–3
servant leaders 36, 98–9
sharing, in supervisory relationship 108–9
Shelton, C. 40–2
Silent Generation *see* Matures
Slade, A. 8–10
Small, T. 96–8
smiling *107*
social awareness 117
status 162, 164
stereotypes, generational 21, 25
stories *see* narrative approach
Strauss, W. 21